Political Communication in the Anglophone World

Political Communication in the Anglophone World

Case Studies

Theodore F. Sheckels

LEXINGTON BOOKS
Lanham • Boulder • New York • Toronto • Plymouth, UK

Published by Lexington Books
A wholly owned subsidiary of The Rowman & Littlefield Publishing Group, Inc.
4501 Forbes Boulevard, Suite 200, Lanham, Maryland 20706
www.rowman.com

10 Thornbury Road, Plymouth PL6 7PP, United Kingdom

British Library Cataloguing in Publication Information Available

Library of Congress Cataloging-in-Publication Data

Political communication in the Anglophone world : case studies / Theodore F. Sheckels
pages cm.
Includes bibliographical references
ISBN 978-0-7391-7078-6 (cloth : alk. paper) — ISBN 978-0-7391-7079-3 (electronic)
1. Communication in politics—Case Studies. 2. Communication in politics—Cross-cultural studies.
I. Title.
JA85.C67 2004
320.917'521014—dc23
2012033860

☉™ The paper used in this publication meets the minimum requirements of American
National Standard for Information Sciences Permanence of Paper for Printed Library
Materials, ANSI/NISO Z39.48-1992.

Printed in the United States of America

Contents

Preface

The impetus for this set of case studies in an absence in extant political communication scholarship. We here in the United States tend to study the United States, both because politics in the United States is our passion and because we feel uneasy studying that in other nations because we— to quote the traveling salesmen at the beginning of *The Music Man*—don't know the territory. I will deal with these concerns in the study's final chapter. Here, by way of preface, let me outline why I think this study is necessary and what I hope it will accomplish. I will also address why I have chosen the case studies I have and why I think I am somewhat qualified to consider these cases.

The absence of work in this area would not justify a study if the area were not worth studying. And, although it should go without saying, political communication is well-worth studying abroad as it is in the United States. Political processes, of course, vary from country to country, and—perhaps—they are freer in the United States than elsewhere. But even if some other nations do not match our level of liberty, they do not totally constrain what the political players say and do. Candidates campaign, and they use media to do so. Political parties position themselves, using media both traditional and new. Those elected as well as those appointed govern. There are speeches, there are debates, there are judicial decisions. The speaking is deliberative, forensic, and epideictic; some of the genres are quite familiar. In other words, there is political communication to study in the other nations of the world and it comes in all of the flavors we are accustomed to seeing and studying in the United States.

Acquiring knowledge of how political communication functions elsewhere ought to, in and of itself, be a worthy scholarly goal, even though that knowledge might not be as relevant in the classroom and in consulting as that of our own country, However, I would suggest that knowing how political communication works abroad can help us see better how it works in the United States. Other countries serve as both mirrors and bases for comparison. Just as earlier campaigns help us understand later ones, communication in one nation can help us better understand communication in ours. (And just as we need to be aware that there are changes with time, we need to be aware that there are changes from nation to nation that will, of course, affect our examination.)

I am hoping then that other political communication scholars will follow suit and embrace what is a very large and largely unexplored area. There have been a few studies, often conducted by scholars with recent or distant connections to a foreign land, but these have been indeed few. Some, fortunately, have been conducted by scholars with valuable foreign language skills—that is, scholars who are sufficiently fluent in German, for example, to grasp the subtleties of political communication in Germany. My focus on the Anglophone world is because, with little Russian and even less French, I could not possibly explore political communication in a language other than English. So, I am hoping that those who follow suit will have the varied language skills necessary to consider political communication in important parts of the world that the vast majority of American communication scholars simply cannot.

Language, then, explains partially why I look at what I look at in this study. The selection of cases is, however, governed by other considerations: a desire to look at a number of countries; a desire to look at a variety of types of communication. But what really drove the selection was the matter of what was intriguing.

Chapters 1 and 2 look north to Canada. The first intriguing story concerns one of Canada's longest-serving prime ministers, Pierre Elliott Trudeau. His long service during rather turbulent times globally and in Canada makes him a good study, but so does his quirkiness. He was able to be multiple people; he was able to seem politically savvy, politically naïve, and politically stupid. He was also quite frequently able to use verbal and nonverbal communication opportunities to take charge and even take a major place on the global stage. Trudeau's life has invited many biographers to attempt to figure out the complex man; the communication he engaged in as a political player should invite the political communication scholar to assess how words, gestures, and media coverage affected the ups and downs of his many years of public service.

The second intriguing Canadian story deals with one of Canada's shortest-serving prime ministers, Kim Campbell. Gender is what makes her story interesting. As the only woman to hold the office, Campbell invites the political communication scholar to ask how she got there and why her stay was so short. Gender issues do indeed affect both her rise and her fall, but they are mixed in with many other issues. One might say that she overcame gender barriers in becoming Tory leader, but she could not overcome the legacy of her Tory predecessor Brian Mulroney once she had to lead the party in a parliamentary election. But as chapter 2 will suggest the story is not that simple. Gender affected both her rise and her fall, just as other issues did.

Chapters 3 and 4 go to the Caribbean, in particular to the island nation of Jamaica. One chapter considers one of its most prominent post-independence political figures, Michael Manley, who served two stints as prime minister. What is intriguing is the difference between "Manley I" and "Manley II." Arguably, the first was a socialist but the second was an advocate of both the free market and somewhat limited government. How did Manley then manage to avoid being lambasted as a "flip-flopper"; how did he convinced the voters that there was a consistency in his message when there seemed to be blatant contradictions?

Manley's long service gained him respect, but the truly revered political figure in Jamaica is reggae artist Bob Marley. To understand Marley's political voice, one has to look at his large body of music. Chapter 4 does so, with an eye to tracing its evolution from a concern for the impoverished people of the "Trench Town" section of Kingston to a concern for all who are African.

Chapter 5 deals generally with sub-Saharan Africa. It considers the communication about this geographic area that both the general public and others, like scholars and political figures, received through the popular media of fiction and film. What images did people acquire about sub-Saharan Africa? Was it accurate? If it was not, along what lines was it distorted? The implication in chapter 5 is that a somewhat distorted image could well have skewed the assessments of political communication scholars and maybe even those in our government responsible for crafting the nation's earliest responses to the emerging postcolonial nations of sub-Saharan Africa. Yes, there were "big men" dictators and plenty of corruption and violence and oppression, but was this the picture, unchanged, from nation to nation throughout a vast region?

The texts considered in chapter 5 deal with Uganda, Nigeria, Ghana, Congo (then Zaire), and South Africa. Chapter 6 deals with another— Kenya. All of the aforementioned nations, with the possible exception of Ghana, have experienced considerable instability over the past several decades. To the contrary, in the postindependence period, Kenya has been quite stable—on the surface. Through the presidencies of Jomo Kenyatta and Daniel arap Moi tribal tensions have percolated beneath the surface. These tensions became more apparent with the election of Mwai Kibaki. The speeches with which he has become his government's leader—inaugurals rhetorically—have borne the burden of uniting a people who had become more obviously divided. Chapter 6 examines how Kibaki has dealt with this and other exigencies of beginning a government in tense times.

Chapters 7, 8, and 9 deal with South Africa. The first two are updated version of essays that appeared in journals. Chapter 8, which considers the rhetoric of Nelson Mandela as president, was originally published in the *Howard Journal of Communications*. It attempts to discern the character of Mandela's rhetoric by using a somewhat quantitative tool, the software program Diction developed by Roderick P. Hart of the University of Texas. This is a dictionary-based program that offers scores on a number of variables in a selected body of discourse. Its application to selected Mandela speeches reveals a disturbing trend away from certainty during the presidency, a trend that had the potential of creating problems for the less charismatic Thabo Mbeki, who would succeed Mandela after his single five-year term as president.

Mbeki did indeed have problems on a number of fronts. Chapter 8 goes back to a very successful moment in Mbeki's political life—a very important address he wrote and delivered while Mandela's vice president. The analysis, originally published in *Communication Quarterly*, reveals Mbeki's use of a mythic narrative echoing the book of Genesis in The Bible as well as echoes of revered American President John F. Kennedy to unite the South African people behind the new African National Congress (ANC) government.

Democratic governments require an opposition. Chapter 9 examines the opposition party that has emerged in South Africa, the Democratic Alliance (DA). Opposing the ANC is risky for several reasons, one being that there is always the possibility of coming across too much like the National Party (NP) that erected apartheid. The chapter examines the DA's website, asking to what extent does the DA seem, presumably inadvertently, too much like the NP. Does the DA, in other words, in crafting an opposition stance, take its rhetoric to a point where retrograde attitudes seem evoked?

Chapters 10 and 11 focus on Australia. Chapter 10 deals with a 1975 "constitutional crisis" when the Governor General, using powers he had but nobody ever thought he would use, dismissed the Labor government led by Gough Whitlam. For a few moments, it looked as if Labor might defy the order, forcing the Governor General to call in troops, who might have refused the Governor General's order and thus defied "The Crown." The events did not take that course; rather, Labor acquiesced, but Whitlam sounded Labor's discontent by an extemporaneous speech as he left the parliament building in Canberra. It is considered a landmark Australian speech. The chapter explores why it is so famous.

Chapter 11 deals with another departure—the fairly recent one of Labor Prime Minister Kevin Rudd after his own party replaced him at its head by Julia Gillard. Using the genre of presidential farewells as a lens, the chapter considers how Rudd's tearful remarks conformed to and departed from the American genre. The chapter attempts to pinpoint Rudd's multiple goals in an address that responds to a complex exigence.

Chapter 12 addresses the methodological issue implicit throughout the case studies. This issue is, fundamentally, can research derived from American political communication and rooted in Western rhetorical theory be used in studying international political communication? The chapter responds by considering the care that is necessary in examining international communication under four somewhat different research situations: first, using the results of empirical studies done in the United States; second, using the procedures defining these empirical studies in studying discourse elsewhere; third, using the results of rhetorically based studies done in the United States; and fourth, using rhetorical theories rooted in Western rhetorical thought. Not surprisingly, the answers to the meta-question at the chapter's core vary from situation to situation.

One examining the case studies will note that the endnotes are fewer than is often the case for political communication studies. Similarly, the bibliography at the book's end does not go on for multiple pages. The basic reason is that there is not much political communication research directly relevant to the case studies. The studies that are referred to tend to be either background information on the case at hand or important studies of American political communication that are providing some of the basis for how the case study proceeds. The studies, then, might look underauthorized. So, let me talk about the background I bring to the book.

I teach and publish on both literature and political communication, for I am a PhD in English who, years ago, drifted into communication studies through the door of coaching speech and debate. My area of literary expertise is what was once called "Commonwealth Literature"—that is, the English-language literature written outside the United Kingdom and the United States. So, the literature courses I still teach deal with Canada, the British Caribbean, British Africa (including South Africa, which had a period of "exile" from The Commonwealth), India, Australia, and New Zealand. I have published two books—plus many essays—dealing with Canadian writing; a book on anti-apartheid South African literature as well as essays in the communication studies discipline on Mandela and Mbeki; and a book on Australia film as well as essays on both film and contemporary fiction. In teaching about and writing on these various Anglophone nations, I have acquired a high level of familiarity with their histories and their cultures. Because I always have an eye on the political, I tend to understand the histories in terms that foreground political matters such as controversial elections, eruptions of discontent, and important public addresses. So, I bring to the cases studies years of careful consideration of these several Commonwealth nations.

Nonetheless, I have tried to tread carefully. Someone in either literature or communication needs to exercise care when talking about political institutions or political history, especially if these are outside one's day-to-day experience of the United States. I constantly asked myself questions such as what would a Canadian think if she read this or a Jamaican if he read that. When I sent my study of the political dimensions of Margaret Atwood's fiction to a Canadian university press, one reviewer responded with a "How dare an American" sentence. Years ago, my study of South African writing received a similar response from an Afrikaner reviewer (although a cheering one from a Zulu reviewer). So, I am very sensitive to the pitfall of assuming that what is true here in politics is true is some other place. Thus, the care.

I do hope that care has prevented errors. But, if there are errors, I suspect that they are on small matters. In other words, I think the readings of the various "texts" that are offered in the case studies ring true even if the explanations of the intricacies of political process or basic historical, geographical facts are slightly off. The goal here, after all, is not to offer the definitive word on eleven political events from all over the Anglophone world but rather to suggest the kind of critical work those in political communication could do and to encourage others to offer not another study of the 2012 American election, but instead an investigation, using whatever method seems appropriate, of the 2012 French one—or even something more esoteric such as the rhetoric surrounding the founding of South Sudan.

I think we political communication scholars can reach beyond the immediate. This book attempts to do so, and it attempts to encourage others to do so.

ONE

Making the Most of the Moments

Pierre Trudeau as Canadian Prime Minister

When one teaches students in the United States about Canada, it is often useful—and revealing—to begin the course by ascertaining what they know about our neighbor to the north. They distressingly cannot name the provinces; they cannot place the major cities on a map. They do slightly better when the question is Canadian musical performers, actors, and hockey teams. But when asked the simplest political question—who is prime minister of Canada, they draw a blank and, then, a few venture as their guess Pierre Trudeau. (In 2012, they still venture this guess!)

This answer suggests something beyond their ignorance of most matters Canadian. It suggests how Trudeau, unlike Canadian leaders since, had an impact on the American consciousness. He was certainly a major Canadian prime minister, but his place in the U.S. consciousness has less to do with the length of his tenure or the accomplishments of his government than the fact that he was a celebrity.

Trudeau is the subject of biographies, histories, and political studies.[1] He and his service as prime minister have been thoroughly discussed—and debated. In some eyes, he was successful in fighting for certain principles; in other eyes, he was the epitome of inconsistency and, thus, a failure. This debate is not one a communication scholar from another country can readily enter into, although, even from abroad, one can note how Trudeau's defenders do succeed in pointing to certain principles he stood for and how his detractors seem to unfairly expect consistency across decades when both changing circumstances and maturation would naturally produce some alterations in Trudeau's positions on public matters. Is it realistic to expect a man who was a radical Quebec nationalist in his youth to stay true to that cause later when it came to

1

mean separatism, not a difficult-to-define special place in a federation? Is it realistic to expect a man to advocate the same policies in a boom economy as in a bust one?

The Trudeau who emerges from all of this scholarly work in different disciplines is a man who adapted; he is also a man whose adaptations often seemed out of sync with the voters. He zigged and zagged, leaving them behind; and, sometimes, being behind translated into very much at odds with Trudeau, ready to reject him and all associated with him. But yet Trudeau frequently regained favor. One is tempted to suggest that the public caught up with Trudeau, and there is some truth to that. However, a better explanation is explored by this chapter. It goes back to why U.S. students even in the second decade of the twenty-first century remember his name: Trudeau was a celebrity. As such, he was covered differently by the media. One night's glance at a television program such as *Entertainment Tonight* would reveal that celebrity coverage is not always positive coverage. And thus it was with Trudeau, but, whether positive, neutral, or negative, the coverage suggested to Canadian voters that they had a "star" at the helm of their government. This suggestion was usually enough to get Trudeau back in favor.

Before this chapter examines how Trudeau repeatedly gained favor, three other topics need to be discussed, for they affect how we comprehend this political career. Those topics are the changes occurring in Canadian and global economics; the changes occurring in Canadian and global media coverage; and exactly what "celebrity" coverage is for a political figure.

First, the economy. The 1960s were a boom time. With economies prospering, tax revenue was high, making possible "Great Society" sorts of programs in many nations. The term is, of course, Lyndon Johnson's, but Canada (and other countries) expanded government services at this same time. When the 1970s arrived, the economy turned sour. Of course, there are always going to be economic ups and downs, but what was going on in the 1970s was at times baffling. Nations such as the United States and Canada had high inflation and high unemployment—thought in theory to be an almost impossible mix, and that theory offered not only few explanations but few solutions. Exacerbating the economic problem were waves of oil price crises. The impact on Trudeau, who became prime minister in 1968, was that he faced not the boom of his predecessor Lester Pearson but economic shocks that voters would at points hold his government accountable for not addressing.

Second, the media. In 1960, the media were still polite and complacent. They were not yet investigative journalists who believed that all aspects of a political figure's life was fair game. The media had not transitioned from lapdogs to attack dogs; the media had not yet been inspired by Woodward and Bernstein's Watergate example to try to expose wrongdoing and bring down governments.[2] But the media were (along

with the times) a-changing. In this changing environment, a political figure such as Trudeau could count on coverage of *both* his political activ-
ities and his personal ones. In fact, one might argue that Trudeau, insofar
as he drew attention to his private life by dressing stylishly and dating a
series of very attractive young women, invited the media to cover both.

Third, "celebrity" coverage. For a political figure, this coverage would
then mix the political and the personal. For both, an emphasis would
probably be placed on what could be seen as well as heard about from a
newsperson. If we think about how programs such as *Entertainment Tonight* cover nonpolitical celebrities, we will note how the stories that have
a visual/aural dimension gain precedence over those that only have the
hosts' reading. The same media tilt is apparent in "celebrity" coverage for
political figures. One implication of this observation is that the political
figures (or their "people") can try to control the coverage. They can steer
the media toward political events they want coverage to focus on; they
can steer the media toward the nonpolitical as well. But both the media
and the politicians are independent agents: there is no guarantee that the
media will go where politicians or their press people steer, and there is
no guarantee that the political figure will do only those nonpolitical
things that the press people judge acceptable. Can they tell someone like
Trudeau whom to date? Whether to dance or not? So, "celebrity" coverage can be controlled, but only to a point. And, as media became less
lapdogs and more attack dogs during the period in question, the coverage became increasingly difficult to control.

EARLY TRUDEAU:
HE SPEAKS, HE WRITES, HE DRESSES WITH FLAIR

Trudeau in the 1940s and 1950s traveled in intellectual circles on the
fringes of the political. In retrospect, one can see how he was gradually
drawn to the political, but that was not the path he was travelling along
in these early decades. With wealth, he had the leisure many did not to
pursue many paths; and travel, the law, and intellectual discussions
emerged as the interests that occupied him. But, in 1942, he gave a spirited speech at a rally for law school classmate Jean Drapeau, who, as an
independent, was seeking a Parliament seat representing an Outremont
riding. It was published, almost in its entirety, in *Le Devoir*. Later, in 1949,
Trudeau gave an even more spirited speech to five thousand miners in
the town of Asbestos. In it, he denounced the Quebec police. In the wake
of both speeches, Trudeau was noticed. Still later, in the early 1950s,
Trudeau wrote, with wit and logic, in *Cite Libre* against the Duplessis
Quebec government. He was further noticed. During this time and afterward, he became noticeable not just for his speaking and his writing but
for "[h]is striking appearance, whimsical yet elegant taste in clothes, and

unpredictability of views" (English, *Citizen*, 300). If you were in early television, you wanted this man on your news and opinion programs: he was striking, and he might say something somewhat outlandish.

Trudeau was at times an eccentric dresser and thus a subject for photographers. But he was not ready to do anything requiring him to mix this image with political action. He wanted to study, he wanted to travel, and he wanted to write. In March 1961, he wrote a strong response to the separatist sentiment that was gathering in Quebec in *Cite Libre*, and in May 1964, he penned for the same publication an impassioned call for reason in politics. These articles were in advance of the turmoil that would break out in the province in 1966.

FINALLY IN GOVERNMENT, BUT "COOL"

Also in advance was the 1965 election. He finally crossed the line from political thinking to political acting as he and two like-minded friends, dubbed by the press the "Three Wise Men," ran for parliamentary seats. Trudeau won what would long prove a safe Mount Royal seat and showed up for work in Ottawa in attire not commonly seen on the rather dour floor of the legislature. Traditionalists such as opposition leader Diefenbaker denounced Trudeau for not showing the revered body due respect; many following the media coverage thought Trudeau's foulard and sandals were "cool."

"TRUDEAUMANIA"

Prime Minister Lester Pearson was probably impressed more with Trudeau's mind than his "cool" attire and gave him increasing responsibilities in the government. The result was that, by 1968, Trudeau had positioned himself as the likely next leader of the Liberals. Quite a feat, many thought, in just three years. Parallel to the sentiment within the government that Trudeau was talented was the sentiment without, fed by increased media coverage, that he had a rock star quality to him. Thus began what the press then and historians since have referred to as "Trudeaumania." The term was derived from the "Beatlemania" that had swept North American and elsewhere mid-decade. Now, as the decade neared its close, Trudeau had become the new John, George, Paul, or Ringo. Media stories highlighted his appearance and his behavior even more than when he was just "cool"; during the campaign for the leadership in 1968 crowds came to see him, not to hear his political ideas.

Several have observed that Trudeau's popularity may be the result of Kennedy envy on the part of Canadians. The United States had elected John F. Kennedy in 1960, and the media covered both his public life and his private life, while still ignoring certain aspects of the latter. Thus was born a "Camelot" that proved very short-lived. Trudeau in 1968 gave Canada its J. F. K. Ironically, another Kennedy, Robert, would give the joyful "Trudeaumania" a jolt. Upon the younger Kennedy's assassination in June, Trudeau attacked his assassin and likened him to the terrorists threatening peace in Quebec. Late in the month, Trudeau rejected advice to skip a parade on Saint-Jean-Baptiste Day that had been forecast to turn riotous. When it did, Trudeau did not flee; rather, he confronted the rioters with a steely stare. He had followed up on his election as Liberal Party leader by gleefully sliding down a bannister at the Chateau Laurier hotel in Ottawa. He thereby showed the playful side people loved. Months later, he stared down pro-separation rioters, showing the courageous side people also loved. And people, thanks to media coverage, saw both sides.

A FOREIGN POLICY ROLLER COASTER

Although most in 1968 would have identified Trudeau as a domestic policy president, he would make more early headlines on foreign policy matters than domestic policy ones. Part of the reason is that the domestic issues in which he was deeply invested were constitutional ones requiring time-consuming paperwork. The other reason is that Trudeau, arguably better-traveled than most Canadian politicians, wanted to express his views on the world. They were views out of sync with what had hitherto dominated Canadian politics. He proposed that Canada pay more attention to the Third World; he suggested that "The West" was overly obsessed with Communism; he argued that U.S. involvement in Vietnam was misguided; and he questioned both the presence of Canadian troops in Europe and the nation's involvement in the NATO alliance. His positions attracted attention and got people thinking, but, then, his position as an enlightened foreign policy thinker was dimmed when he responded to news of civil warfare in West Africa by publicly asking, "Where's Biafra," and, then, maintaining a Canadian connection to apartheid South Africa well after many other nations had adopted sanctions.

Down in popularity because of media coverage of his African gaffes, Trudeau went up when he appealed to anti-monarchist attitudes in Canada by balking at attending the 1969 meeting of Commonwealth nations, reluctantly going, and—in a reprise of his Chateau Laurier frolicking— sliding down a banister in Buckingham Palace within sight of a not-very-pleased Elizabeth I. The media moment established Trudeau as willing to question old ways, old ties. He followed through in the next eighteen months by extending diplomatic recognition to Communist China and ordering that no nuclear weapons would henceforth be carried on Canadian military aircraft.

RESPONDING TO TERRORISM IN QUEBEC

His stock up, Trudeau responded to politically inspired kidnappings in Quebec. He not only refused to negotiate but he called for the invocation of the War Measures Act. Parliament approved his call with only sixteen dissenting votes; public opinion concurred with only 5 percent disapproval. Defiant, yes; irreverent, yes. But he perhaps pushed the latter too far when he responded in parliamentary debate with John Lundrigan over the War Measures Act invocation by quietly mouthing the "F word." He later joked that what he had really mouthed had been "fuddle duddle." People laughed; people joked; but they also began to develop a feeling that perhaps their charismatic prime minister was not always serious enough.

RESPONDING TO ECONOMIC CRISES

What really hurt Trudeau's popularity was less his "fuddle duddle" moment than the souring Canadian economy. The Liberal government simply did not know how to respond. Somewhat frozen by the crisis with internal division between pro-business and pro-labor wings, the Liberals allowed the New Democratic Party to outflank it on the left, almost resulting in an election loss in 1972. The Liberals thereafter drifted left, securing its base, but the party was still on shaky ground until an interprovincial dispute handed Trudeau the opportunity to score points in eastern Canada and a Tory misstep handed Trudeau the opportunity to pit his political enemies against each other.

With the early 1970s came the first oil crisis. Prices began soaring in most of Canada, and lines at gasoline stations got longer and longer. Alberta, however, was a producer of oil and could alleviate the problem. Alberta, however, wanted the new market value for its oil, no matter whether the province sold it abroad or in Ontario and Quebec. The dispute became almost as serious a threat to the union as separatist sentiment in Quebec. Trudeau sided with the eastern provinces, renewing his popularity east of the Canadian shield.

There was still, in the early to mid 1970s, the threat of inflation. Believing it to be perceived by the public as the major threat, the Tories entered the 1974 election calling for wage and price controls. The New Democratic Party angrily attacked the Tories. On the sidelines somewhat, against controls but not vehemently so, stood Trudeau and the Liberals. With popularity in the east and with the NDP attacking the Tories, Trudeau and the Liberals won an easy victory. They celebrated with an elaborate picnic for 100,000 on Toronto Island, an event covered extensively in the media, which emphasized how many people were present celebrating the victory of their celebrity prime minister.

SPEAKING OUT AGAINST CAPITAL PUNISHMENT

The economic problems facing the nation persisted, sending Trudeau's stock downward. But a magnificent public address in July 1976 on capital punishment reversed the decline. He argued that Canada should abolish it. Notwithstanding the fact that capital punishment was favored by 69 percent of the voters, his eloquence resulted in a 130-124 vote on abolition in the legislature. The media coverage of the address and the vote earned Trudeau support. That support was, however, short-lived: a principled victory on a matter of civil liberty could not trump the enduring economic problems.

MARITAL PROBLEMS

The economic problems were not the only ones facing Trudeau. The media had always paid attention to the prime minister's love life: the women he dated, the courtship of the much younger Margaret Sinclair, and his marriage to her and the rapid growth of the Trudeau family. Initially, it was a story that fit the Camelot frame. However, marital problems eventually became noticeable. In retrospect, we realize that Margaret was suffering from a form of bipolar disorder, resulting in frenzied periods of seemingly joyful activity followed by episodes of deep depression. At the time, many simply thought that Margaret was dissatisfied with the life of a prime ministers's wife. She wanted more freedom than that life provided; she wanted more of husband Pierre's time.

The marital difficulties initially affected Trudeau adversely. They ran contrary to the Camelot story and, thus, were detrimental to Trudeau's appeal as "JFK-North." However, when it became clear that Margaret was more of the problem than Pierre, the public's attitude shifted. Had he been an inattentive husband, the fault would have been his—to his personal and political detriment. However, Margaret advertised her feelings in a manner too public—in her partying and in her published confessing. She was not being the good wife, and, perhaps more important, she was not being the good mother of three.

CONFRONTING QUEBEC SEPARATISM

Trudeau perhaps capitalized on that upsurge of sympathy in a speech, a gesture, and another speech in the 1977 to 1978 period. Although economic difficulties persisted, Trudeau maintained considerable support. So, he began dealing with growing separatist sentiment in Quebec from a position of strength.

The first address was delivered to the U.S. Congress. This speech was presented by the media as a response to nationalist Rene Levesque's challenge in Quebec. Trudeau spoke firmly: yes, the Quebec agitation for independence was the major Canadian problem, he told the Congress, but his government was committed and would fight for no further decentralization in the Canadian federation and no special status for Quebec within it. Trudeau, francophone and from Quebec, would not bow to Levesque's demands or his rhetoric.

FOREIGN AFFAIRS: IRREVERENCE AND IDEALISM

The strong Trudeau was also the playfully defiant Trudeau. At a state dinner in London, irked at the protocol that treated heads of state separately from those, such as himself, who were technically not in that exalted category, he performed an elegant pirouette after the Queen had exited. The precise meaning of his gesture was difficult to discern, but it clearly was meant to signal that those relegated to a lesser status by protocol were not going to recede into the palace woodwork.

In addition to strength and playful defiance, Trudeau also signaled forward thinking in a United Nations address. Here, he questioned the world's reliance on nuclear weaponry. This was 1978, two years before Ronald Reagan defeated Jimmy Carter and, after inauguration, took a hard line toward the Soviet Union and worked to restore the United States' nuclear strength. Trudeau was very clearly thinking along very different lines than Reagan.

POST-1980 ELECTION: A RENEWED TRUDEAU

The economy continued to weigh down the Liberals. Polls showed Trudeau popular but the party was not. His personal popularity—some of it sympathy because Margaret was partying the nights away at trendy New York nightclubs—was not, however, sufficient to prevent the party's defeat in 1979. The province-by-province vote for 1979 will prove to be instructive, for it revealed that the Liberals had alienated western Canada. That alienation proved not to be an issue, however, in 1980, when a revitalized Trudeau led the Liberals to victory. That victory, however, was won with a phenomenally high Liberal vote in Quebec and a very strong one in Ontario. In other words, Trudeau now led a very much regional party whose victory was largely because it was so very strong in its region and its region was very populous.

Trudeau, now in a second political life, aggressively pursued three important issues: a resolution to the Quebec issue; a new Canadian constitution with a bill of rights; what he would probably describe as a liberal foreign policy agenda featuring nuclear disarmament and more attention on the part of the developed nations to the less-developed ones. He would be able to pursue the first two while sustaining his political strength.

Trudeau vs. Levesque

Trudeau would overtly challenge Levesque, and win. He would win rhetorically when he used the occasion of Levesque's attack that mocked Trudeau's Anglophone middle name "Elliot" to lambast Levesque, making the Quebecois leader look decidedly "small." He would win at the referendum that brought 85.61 percent of eligible voters to the polling place. The battle had turned into a personal one between Trudeau and Levesque. As such, it was the kind of story the media wanted. That coverage gave Trudeau additional *ethos* for the battle over the proposed constitution and bill of rights.

The Constitution and Bill of Rights

The story of the constitution is a complicated one, one that began long before Trudeau became prime minister in 1968 and continued after his 1984 retirement. There were many issues. The basic one—put simply— was the extent to which federalism would be permitted to go or, conversely, how strong the central government would be permitted to be. Trudeau's position, despite his roots in Quebec and his very early embracing of Quebec nationalism, was for a fairly strong central government. Quebec and Alberta wanted not just federalism, but some kind of special status in the federation for their provinces. Each had, in the judgment of some Quebec and Alberta political leaders, special issues that required special consideration: language and culture in the case of Quebec; oil in the case of Alberta. Trudeau's initial approach was negotiation, which proved unending. Thus, on October 2, 1980, he delivered an eloquent speech calling for the parliament to patriate the constitution. The speech, which attracted considerable media attention, prompted, not a vote, but further negotiations, which, eventually, led to a compromise that Trudeau celebrated as good for the nation. His opponents began grumbling about the compromise they had agreed to shortly after agreeing. So, Trudeau won. However, that victory would later be challenged.

The National Energy Program

In the midst of the debate over the constitution in fall 1980, Trudeau's government proposed the National Energy Program (NEP). That Trudeau proposed it was to his credit in the eyes of media in eastern Canada. There, his stock rose. In Alberta (and other places), his popularity, already low, declined still farther. Alberta saw the NEP as an attack on both its business interests and its sovereignty and was determined to fight. The media loved the idea: it was a fight pitting East versus West, Trudeau versus Alberta leader Lougheed, poor versus rich. The fight fizzled. If Trudeau had earned something like points in the eyes of the public in the 1980 election and in his defeat of Levesque, he seemed to have spent them all on a battle over the constitution that was not as attractive to the media as the fight over energy costs. When it came time to push the NEP forward, Trudeau seemed once more in decline—done in, again, largely by economic problems his party had not yet figured out because the symptoms continued to defy traditional theories. So, when Queen Elizabeth visited Canada in 1982, Trudeau was in decline. His repeat of his pirouette—this time at the airport upon her departure—did not have the effect his previous one did. Media did cover it, but, at best, the gesture kept Trudeau from hitting bottom. The media were, in fact, puzzled as to how to read the Trudeau gesture.

SEEKING INTERNATIONAL LEGACY

In these last years of Trudeau's service as prime minister, the economic problems were intractable. Whether or not conservatives had an answer, time would tell, but, for the moment, Trudeau was left with the international stage on which to achieve whatever coverage and whatever good effects he might. In these years, he insisted on a Canadian presence at the highest level of international discussions. From that position, he served as a counterpoint to the dominant Reagan-Thatcher viewpoint that was dominating such discussions, creating some tension between both these two leaders and Trudeau and their nations and Canada. Trudeau's voice was not, however, one to be pushed aside: he would be heard, and his agenda would be acknowledged. He was allowed to arrange meetings— most notably, one in Cancun—where North-South issues would be explored in depth. There, still fashionable, he was often photographed, but, given the lack of interest in these issue on the parts of Reagan and Thatcher, the best he could achieve were polite nods and photo opportunities. Media coverage, yes, but meaningful action to help developing nations, no. Trudeau did though, perhaps, actually persuade many on another of his foreign affairs causes—the need for nuclear disarmament. One of his last speeches that acquired significant media coverage, an October 28, 1983, address in Guelph, called in strong language for the extant nuclear powers to reduce their armaments. He then began a world tour to promote this anti-nuclear cause. Some invited Trudeau; some did not. Some supported him; some did not. But he made headlines. Finally, at a December NATO ministerial meeting, he gained agreement that the group would meet in January in Stockholm to discuss the disarmament issue as well as a declaration, over British and American objections, supporting détente. On the North American side of the Atlantic, Trudeau's message may have eventually swayed Reagan or his advisors to at least try to reverse the arms race. The historic 1986 meeting in Iceland between Reagan and Gorbachev may have been born in Trudeau's global advocacy and in his private conversations at the White House with Reagan in mid-December 1983. Thatcher, on the other side of the Atlantic, never warmed to Trudeau or his message.

CELEBRATING A POLITICAL CELEBRITY: HE DID IT HIS WAY

Trudeau's diplomatic work, both because it was noble and quite visible, did raise his popularity back in Canada. However, the country's economic woes quickly caused it to fall. So, Trudeau decided that the best course of action for him to take would be to end his political career. He did so, however, in a grand manner that made him a celebrity politician one more time. There was a twenty-minute biofilm that struck some observers as a rock video because of its score and its portrayal of the flashy Trudeau. Then, there were many tributes by both political figures and Hollywood ones. Then, with the arena darkened, Trudeau took the stage and delivered an eloquent farewell. Then, Canadian Paul Anka sang an edited version of Sinatra's "My Way." It celebrated a politician who always did things "His Way."

Doing things "His Way" was thought by many at the time to be an apt description of Trudeau's career. From a communication perspective, doing things "His Way" often created the very moments of celebrity coverage that affected his career. In fact, one could argue that his doing things "His Way" gave some of those moments the qualities that attracted the celebrity coverage. Whether Trudeau stood his ground, spoke his mind, performed a pirouette, slid down a bannister, or dressed in style, Trudeau was enacting politics as he saw fit. Whether he was arrogantly irreverent or defiantly principled, he had enough of the "rock star" in his demeanor to gain media attention based on the enactment itself as much as whatever political issue might directly or indirectly be involved.

Trudeau was long-serving, and his accomplishments as prime ministers are many. True, he did not accomplish as much as he would have liked. Some of the issues he wrestled with, such as the constitution, were extremely complicated ones: on these he made progress. Some involved global players whom he could only hope to influence. And he did, establishing an international presence for Canada that it had not had before. But economic and energy problems constantly held Trudeau back. His answers to these problems were not inspired, but the other political parties had no better ones. And neither did other international players. Thus, the issues persisted and probably would have hurt whichever party was in power. That Trudeau survived the dips in popularity that the economic and energy crises prompted is a tribute to the celebrity coverage he received. His speeches, his actions, his style, and many dimensions of his personal life drew media coverage, and much of that coverage improved his political fortunes.

NOTES

1. John English's excellent two-volume biography of Trudeau is the source for much of factual information in this discussion of Trudeau. There are several biographies of Trudeau in print, but English's struck me as having an objectivity lacking in other treatments of the prime minister. He is indeed both revered and reviled in Canada it would seem based on the positive-negative range the published work on Trudeau takes. My view here tilts in a more positive direction. As a corrective, one might look at Laxer and Laxer's study, which focuses on what the authors argue to be Trudeau's poor responses to the nation's economic difficulties, or McDonald's, which deals more with Trudeau personally and argues that his pride stood in the way of effective government.

2. The canine terms of, of course, Larry Sabato's in *Feeding Frenzy: Attack Journalism and American Politics* (Baltimore: Lanahan, 2000).

TWO

Kim Campbell and Gender

The question of a woman holding the office of the U.S. presidency has, of course, been raised in many articles and several books.[1] Frequently in these scholarly and popular treatments, the authors note that women have achieved the highest political position in other Western democracies—the United Kingdom, Germany, and Ireland, for example. They might also note Canada, although they might not, for Kim Campbell's time at the top was very brief. If one is trying to contrast the success of women elsewhere with their failure in the United States, the case of Kim Campbell may not be one that attention should be focused on. However, if the focus is not the contrast but, rather, the similar barriers women in politics face, then the story of Kim Campbell is well worth attending to, for her comparative success may well be misleading. Campbell's difficulties, partially caused by gender but partially caused by a host of other political factors, may recall problems women have faced and forecast problems political women will face in the United States.

Kim Campbell's story is worth attending to not because her story is ultimately one of failure to surmount the barriers but precisely because it is a complex one. As this chapter will demonstrate, Campbell did seem to be disadvantaged at points in her campaign because of her gender. However, as is true in most political stories, gender was not *the* issue. There are many reasons why she won her campaign to be leader of the Conservative Party (and, thus, Prime Minister) just as there are many reasons why she lost the election she called shortly after assuming office. Gender is part of the mix, and this chapter will tease that part out in order to suggest how gender prejudice does indeed insinuate itself in political campaigns in which no one explicitly raises the issue. Certainly, behind the scenes, women supporting Campbell may have said women should support her because of her gender; and, undoubtedly, behind the scenes, some men uttered misgivings because of that fact. However, in neither election was gender as prominent an issue as in, for example, Hillary Clinton's 2008 campaign for the U.S. presidency. Nonetheless, as this chapter will demonstrate, the issue was present. People did not talk about a "glass ceiling," but one did hover over Campbell.

The chapter, first, needs to differentiate Campbell's two elections from the U.S. experience. Although the chapter will ultimately argue that the differences are not crucial when the focus is on the question of gender, readers still need to understand that neither 1993 race is like what the United States sees and, thus, what most research is tied to.

The first 1993 race was for party leadership. In the United States, there are party leaders in both houses of Congress, and they are elected by the houses' respective members. There is internal campaigning, and the media do cover it. However, especially since most of the campaigning is one-on-one in difficult-to-study conversations, media coverage is inherently limited.

In Canada, there is a single party leader, and his or her election is a much more public affair. Once it is apparent that there will be an opening, rumors begin circulating about who is interested in the office and who is not. At some point, those truly interested will announce their candidacy, but their campaign work has usually begun before this public point. Their supporters try to build up party membership with like-minded voters with an eye to acquiring a numerical advantage when delegates to the party's convention are selected, for a party convention will ultimately select the leader. This convention is much like American nominating conventions insofar as there are nominating speeches, demonstrations, and multiple ballots. Ballots do occur, differentiating the Canadian convention from recent American ones at which voting never goes beyond round one. However, the crucial difference is that, in Canada, each candidate has a finite opportunity to address the convention before the balloting begins. The candidates, all of them, have an opportunity for a final, perhaps crucial campaign address.

Before the convention convenes, there is national campaigning. Much of it centers on meetings between the prospective leaders and delegates; however, there is also an attempt to sway the delegates by swaying the larger population. Thus, there is a sequence of televised "debates" among the candidates. Recognizing that a "debate" is difficult when there are many candidates, those organizing the 1993 events termed them "policy forums." Truth be told, like the "debates" during the U.S. primary seasons, they floated in a gray area between being debates and being discussions. This situation disadvantaged Campbell because, as frontrunner, she was the target of most remarks that might be termed attacks and was trapped in a format that did not permit immediate responses on her part unless she should violate the norms and interject such a response out of turn.[2] This disadvantage is, of course, one any frontrunner would experience, but, as this chapter will later note, her gender constrained her further in these debates, for she was very conscious of not coming across as overly aggressive, for aggression in a woman is viewed differently than aggression in a man.[3]

The second 1993 race was, ostensibly, for parliamentary seats. Thus, much of the campaigning was between or among the candidates in particular ridings. The party leader, however, has a major role in Canadian parliamentary elections: he or she is to lead the party's campaign effort. This means that he or she speaks to audiences of various sizes and compositions, talks with editorial boards, and debates throughout the nation. Some events are in particular ridings because the seat there is at-risk or the member there is especially important to the party or the leader; other events are part of a national campaign's strategic plan to make the leader visible throughout the country while, perhaps, targeting certain provinces or parts of provinces that are thought vital to the overall effort.

The second race is peculiar when viewed from an American point of view. The election certainly looks and feels like one for the office of prime minister. Thus, it is strikingly like a U.S. presidential race. However, the election is for parliamentary seats, the mathematics of which will determine who the prime minister will be. One implication of the race that can escape notice if it is viewed as being like a U.S. presidential race is that the leader, because of the expectation that he or she will lead the party's effort, will possibly neglect campaigning in his or her own riding. Thus, it is advisable that a leader come from a "safe" riding so that its neglect does not become a political embarrassment.

Before this chapter turns to the two 1993 campaigns with the question of gender foremost in mind, the reader also needs some background information on Kim Campbell.[4] The most important piece of information is that she is a Tory—that is, a member of the nation's Conservative Party. Pundits and scholars alike have commented that a woman's chance to be elected in the United States probably declines the more she is found by the electorate to be "liberal." If the same is true in Canada—and I would suggest it is—then Campbell's chances of cracking the proverbial "glass ceiling" would be enhanced by her party affiliation. Now, in Canada as elsewhere, not all members of a political party are identical. Campbell's conservatism was evident on economic issues more than others. On social issues, especially so-called women's issues, she was perhaps more attuned to the Liberal Party's positions; however, she exhibited a caution on such issues that made her both acceptable to Tories and barely acceptable to many women who wanted her to take a stronger position on women's role in society. She, then, walked a political tightrope: should she crusade for women, she would lose Tory support; should she not object to sexism when she saw or experienced it, she would lose women's support. And, as the reader will see, she needed women's support in the parliamentary election because she needed more support than the Conservative Party, as she inherited it from Brian Mulroney, could muster. The outgoing Mulroney had left her with a weak party, although Mulroney's closest advisors did not seem to grasp this political reality.

Campbell is also from Canada's West—specifically, British Columbia. The Conservative Party was historically dominated by the "Big Blue Machine" in Ontario. Because it is proverbial in Canada that you cannot win a parliamentary election without winning Quebec, the Tories had catered to that province, thus creating, in the nation's Mideast, a Tory stronghold. This stronghold did not exclude Conservatives from the Maritimes or from the West; however, it did situate them, for ill or good, outside the party mainstream. The "ill" side is that they were viewed suspiciously as having independent views somewhat out of sync with the mainstream and thus afforded lukewarm support by the party hierarchy; the "good" side is that they had sufficient independence to stake out somewhat different positions that reflected their provinces' different situations. Alberta, for example, Tory Prime Minister Joe Clark's province, was an oil producer with a different agenda on energy questions than other provinces. British Columbia, Campbell's province, was—arguably—more involved in Pacific trade, more international in perspective, and more eco-friendly than other areas. The ability to stake out somewhat different positions can lead to party disunity, but, if the party needs—as the Conservatives did in 1993—to go beyond the shrinking constituency that had defeated the Liberal Trudeau and brought the Conservative Mulroney to power, then the ability to say new or different things can be an asset.

Americans need to be aware that provinces are not just larger version of the U.S. states. Rather, they are political entities with a striking degree of independence from the central government in Ottawa. This independence creates a pronounced provincial identity for political figures. It also, as the previous chapter suggests, creates testy debates over the precise nature of Canadian federalism. Campbell's being a Westerner, thus, was far more important politically than Barack Obama's being from Illinois or John McCain's being from Arizona in 2008. The closest the United States comes to the Canadian provincial identity may be with politicians who hail from Texas: many Americans do, without perhaps interrogating the belief, grant Texans a more pronounced state-based identity than politicians from most other U.S. states.

Finally, it is useful to know that Campbell, at the time she came to the political fore in these two campaigns, was twice divorced and not married. The very fact that she was at the fore despite these personal facts suggests that the political climate in Canada was more open in 1993 than it once was. Once, such facts would have disqualified a man or a woman from high office. The political climate, however, may have opened up more quickly for males than for females, meaning that her marital history could still evoke negative comments from some. In addition, she not only lacked a supporting spouse during the campaigns, but, in the later campaign, had a gentleman friend whom she was seeing. This relationship could create insinuations from both within the party and from the opposition. Campbell notes as much in her memoirs.

Campbell's political career could, of course, be reviewed here in some detail, but these are the essential facts to know about her before considering the dynamics of the two 1993 campaigns. These plus the fact of her gender. As if to highlight that, one almost comical event occurred less than a year before the initial 1993 campaign. Earlier, Campbell had posed for photographer Barbara Woodley, who was preparing a book entitled *Portraits* that would feature prominent Canadian women. Campbell's portrait was shot with her wearing a strapless evening gown. In 1992, Woodley was exhibiting these portraits at the National Arts Centre in Ottawa. The *Ottawa Citizen* reproduced the bare-shouldered Campbell in its coverage. This prompted Member of Parliament (MP) Lynn Hunter to compare Campbell to the American pop star Madonna, which prompted the British press to run the photograph with the caption "The Madonna of Canada." (The Italian press, mistranslating "bare shoulders," reported that Campbell had posed with nude men!) Comic, yes, but the incident also shows how very quickly Campbell's gender could take center stage, making all that one might say about a lengthy political career involving local, provincial, and federal experience seem irrelevant.

CAMPAIGNING FOR PARTY LEADER

Conservative Prime Minister Brian Mulroney was serving his second mandate. For reasons that need not be explored here, his popularity with voters was waning. Many were asking themselves if he would lead the Tories into another election or if he would retire before that election had to occur. Mulroney was giving mixed signals, but more signals suggested retirement than another (probably unsuccessful) campaign. So, behind the scenes, there was both speculation about who would be a candidate for party leader should he step down and some early, informal campaigning. Campbell had made a name for herself in cabinet by managing the justice portfolio quite well. She was now managing the defense portfolio and thereby gaining expertise in international affairs. Her name was mentioned by many during this speculative phase, and, yes, she did have conversations with some in which she explored the possibility of running for party leader should Mulroney decide to step down. In so doing, she was acting as were others with an interest in the leadership position.

Initially, the field seemed relatively wide open, and Campbell was not the only woman whose name was frequently mentioned during this "surfacing" phase. Without indicting Mulroney or explicitly questioning the stability of the Quebec-West coalition he had assembled, many thought the party had to offer voters a new vision to be successful in 1993. In some minds, a female candidate would help the party do so. A female at the helm would signal "new"; in addition, her presence would possibly attract women voters to the party, adding new voters to compensate for others who Mulroney, because of his policies or his manner of governing, had turned off. Campbell initially talked about her candidacy with her fellow MP's from British Columbia. MP Mary Collin, initially noncommittal, after asking Campbell to explain how she planned to increase popular involvement in decision-making, finally endorsed her and offered to head-up the campaign's outreach efforts to women members and delegates. Her offering suggests how Campbell's candidacy, from the outset, had a gendered dimension. In a sense, Campbell was becoming the woman's candidate, not just the woman candidate.

Campbell herself was concerned about controversial positions she had taken in the past on social issues; she was also concerned about her ability to gain support in Ontario and Quebec. As Campbell considered her liabilities, prominent candidates began dropping out of the race. Perhaps they knew that Mulroney's successor would have a difficult time winning an election given the Prime Minister's declining popularity and the absence of a galvanizing issue such as free trade that might hold the Mulroney coalition together. Among those who dropped out was Ontario MP Barbara McDougall, finally clearing the way for Campbell to be *the* female candidate. She was increasingly covered by the media as such. The media people who began paying attention to Campbell were the political campaign reporters in what seems to be a very specialized media. As such, they had relatively limited information on Campbell. They had media colleagues who had extensively covered Campbell's work while she held the justice portfolio. However, such was the structure of the media business, that what reporters covering justice knew never made it to the reporters covering campaigns. When Jean Charest, the environment minister who would eventually become Campbell's chief rival for the leadership, officially declared his candidacy, he went on the radio in Montreal demanding to know "one thing that Ms. Campbell stands for." He could not have made that demand had it not been for the fact that the media projected a lack of awareness of her record as justice minister and her stances—some controversial—on a number of social issues. The political reporters presented Campbell—peculiarly—as "new," as something of a blank slate, when, in fact, she had a considerable record of both positions on issues and achievements as a minister.

Campbell did not like speaking to a large audience from a text; she preferred delivering a public address from notes she herself had prepared. Her preference fits gendered norms, but it also puts her at a disadvantage with regards to media coverage. Reporters prefer a text that they can immediately use and do not like waiting for a transcript to be produced. She wanted her audience to understand that the words were hers, not ones that had been handed her. She also wanted the freedom to make eye contact with her auditors. Campbell, thus, always resisted being scripted. When she was not successful, supporters sometimes screamed, "Let Kim be Kim," causing her to resist scripts even more. She successfully resisted when she made her official candidacy declaration speech. In that speech, she seemed to have two rhetorical goals: first, to let people know who Kim Campbell was (since the media was not informing them); second, to establish herself as the candidate of inclusion. To accomplish the latter goal, she highlighted two facts about herself that sometimes, she said, made her painfully aware of what it felt like to be politically excluded: the fact that she was from British Columbia and the fact that she was a woman.

Before her official announcement, her media coverage was positive but vague. After the announcement, the media's tone changed. Campbell characterized the next-day interviewing behavior of Peter Mansbridge and Pamela Wallin of CBC TV's *Prime Time News* as "verg[ing] on outright rudeness."[5] Were they upset that she had not given the media an advanced text of her address? Or had her story, from the reporters' point-of-view changed? Before her announcement, she was the intriguing prospect that they wanted to dangle (vaguely) before viewers; now, she was a candidate to be leveled by watchdog or junkyard dog journalism.

Ahead of her, along with a defense portfolio that required much travel, was a series of debates or policy forums with the other five official candidates. The party, to stress collegiality among the fellow conservatives, tried to present these events as discussions. The media did not follow suit: they wanted confrontation. The media also now recalled information about Campbell that they had forgotten—not her positions or her record but that she could be arrogant and abrasive. They recalled this information because it gave them information to fill in the confrontational frame they were using for the debates. At the initial debate on April 15 in Toronto, the candidates differed as to whether they accepted the party's framing or the media's framing, resulting in some confusion as to how to execute the format. Was the forum a discussion or a confrontation? How were they to take turns in an orderly group discussion if the event degenerated into attacks demanding immediate responses?

As the frontrunner in the race, Campbell became the target of attacks. Thus, the confusing format hurt her more than Charest and the others. In addition, she confessed afterward that the studio lights were giving her a headache and standing in her two-inch heals was causing her pain. Still, immediate polling showed she and Charest tied with the viewing public. Media spin, however, quickly turned a tie into a disastrous loss for Campbell. The media had found—perhaps developed through its framing, which positioned her as a candidate to be brought down—the event to level her.

Given how Charest's succinct (arguably superficial) answers had fared better with the media than her attempts to discuss issues, she shifted to Charest's strategy for the April 21 French language debate in Montreal. The campaign staff, which was experiencing internal tensions between "Big Blue Machine" Tories and "Young Turks" (who disliked all that the "Big Blue Machine" stood for), tried to give Campbell advice on clothing color and hair style. She was told to wear pastels and to die the roots of her blondish hair brown. She deflected most of this advice, concentrating on responding directly to attacks. She fared better with the media in the Montreal debate, although her responses were labeled "soft." Would she have fared better with the media if she has been more aggressive, or would the media have taken the aggression as proof that she was indeed *too* aggressive. She was trapped in a double-bind. And was she the media's target just because she was the frontrunner? And was Charest being told to alter his attire or hair? Campbell indeed had to wonder at this point about the extent to which her treatment by both the media and her well-intended campaign was gendered.

Campbell could not reflect long on such questions, for her duty as defense minister had thrust her into the midst of a controversy. There had been what one military official described as a complete breakdown of discipline among Canadian troops deployed on a peacekeeping mission in Somalia resulting in the mysterious death of a civilian while in custody and the equally mysterious attempted suicide of a Canadian soldier who had been on guard. Campbell, as former justice minister, knew that she might be involved in some manner in the adjudication of a crime; therefore, she proceeded cautiously in making public comments. Meanwhile, the Chief of the Defense Staff, Admiral John Anderson, spoke freely to the media. The result was that the media and political opponents accused Campbell of trying to cover up the Somalia incident. This accusation weakened her candidacy, and it lingered beyond the leadership campaign into the later parliamentary campaign. Pollsters even then found voters opposed to Campbell's party because she covered up the embarrassing events in Somalia.

Three more debates to go. Campbell fared well in Calgary on April 30. But in Vancouver on May 13, she seemed to echo Brian Mulroney's derisive comment on opponents of a new Constitution when she characterized those who were trying to ignore the deficit as "the enemies of Canadians." The media were very quick to link her to the unpopular Mulroney. But that media treatment was nothing compared to that on May 18 when radio and television alike picked up on a *Toronto Star* story that claimed, "Kim Campbell says she got converted Anglican to ward off the demons of the papacy."[6] The story's author, Patrick Doyle, had evidently been encouraged to expose this and other Campbell "secrets" by the Charest campaign.

Campbell's team released the full text of an interview with journalist Peter Newman that Doyle had cited. Then, after the press had had the opportunity to read the text, Campbell's team called a press scrum. The result was several articles denouncing the Doyle story. Newman took to the air to defend Campbell and denounce Doyle's story. Few, however, criticized Doyle himself, let alone inquired as to his motivation in writing the piece. The Charest campaign was silent about the event.

Campbell and Charest by this point were far ahead of other candidates. If the media's game was simply to expose the foibles of those in the lead, why then was Campbell always the target, Charest never? Perhaps he and his campaign handled media relations better. Still, there seemed bias in the coverage. Every slip by Campbell was magnified, and the media still acted as if Campbell had no record and no policy positions. Ross Howard of the *Globe and Mail* asked, in print, what Campbell stood for, totally ignoring the multipage "Proposals for Democratic Reform" that the Campbell campaign had just issued. Lysiane Gagnon, political columnist for *La Presse*, diagnosed the media situation facing Campbell in detail in a June 5 op-ed piece in the *Globe and Mail*. She pointed to the many ways in which Campbell had been the victim of media bias: being accused of being ambitious when no more so than Charest, being caught in a double-bind between styles labeled either too soft or too aggressive, having every gaffe magnified when Charest's were all ignored or dismissed.

The media, however, were only a part of Campbell's problem. Her campaign, as already noted, had attracted many experienced operatives from Ontario's "Big Blue Machine." They not only pushed aside the "Young Turks" who wanted political reform, but marginalized the many women drawn to the Campbell campaign because of its historic importance for women in Canadian politics. The result was that little attention was paid to events that might attract women to the Campbell candidacy. Some of this marginalization was undoubtedly accidental: the "BBM" men knew how to run a campaign; they had run many, many before. However, some was probably intentional because they did not want to give the campaign a "feminist" feel for fear that such a feel might turn off antifeminist elements in the party. They evidently felt there were some.

And, if problems with the media and problems within the campaign were not enough, members of the Liberal Party were also criticizing Campbell's work as a minister. The Liberals knew they could win in the next election unless Mulroney's replacement was able to attract new members to the conservative cause. Only Campbell among the candidates for Tory leader had this potential, so they were intent upon keeping her from becoming Mulroney's successor. Therefore, they tried to keep defense issues—and Tory mishandling of them—in the news.

Toward the campaign's end, future Tory prime minister Joe Clark, a Charest supporter, suggested that Campbell might not have the "stability" necessary for the job. His wife Maureen opined that Campbell's not having children meant that she did not have as much invested in the future as had Charest. MP Terry Clifford, a Charest supporter, suggested that Canadians would identify more with Charest than with Campbell because he had a wife and children and, thus, formed a photogenic family. MP Bill McKnight, a Charest supporter, went so far as to compare Campbell's supporters with Jim Jones's suicidal followers in Jonestown. These late views, which lacked the subtlety of earlier instances of sexism, actually may have backfired on the Charest campaign, for, once the convention began, prominent women in the party who had thus far remained neutral, chose to support Campbell because of what one characterized as the orchestrated "anti-woman tone" of the Charest campaign.

The Campbell campaign managed the convention quite well: her colors were everywhere; her supporters always in prime positions. Kim Campbell herself gave a creditable speech. It was scripted—it had to be because of time constraints, so Campbell felt it was flatter than her more extemporaneous offerings. Nonetheless, it held her support firm, and, although she failed by 71 votes on the initial ballot, she picked up 153 between that ballot and the second and was proclaimed the new leader of the Conservative Party and, for the moment, prime minister.

That victory should not, however, obscure two conclusions. First, she experienced the scrutiny and setbacks all political candidates experience. Second, she arguably experienced them more because of her gender.

CAMPAIGNING FOR PARLIAMENTARY MAJORITY

When campaigning for party leader, you are campaigning for yourself. Those who become convention delegates may be asking how you will do as party leader in the next election: they may occasionally glance at that bigger picture. Nonetheless, their gaze is upon the arrayed individuals who have stepped forward as potential leaders. The first 1993 campaign then was about Kim Campbell; the second 1993 campaign will be less about her and more about the Conservative Party. Campbell will, of course, be the face of the party. Thus, the question becomes can what she stands for come to define the party enough for voters to elect as MPs men and women from that party or will what the party has stood for prior to her ascent be dominant in voters' minds. The question, then, is less about Kim Campbell as individual and more about the symbolic message she might convey. Given this, one would expect sexism to be less of an issue in the parliamentary campaign than in the leadership one. The sexism probably was diminished, but it was far from nonexistent.

The campaign per se began, of course, when Prime Minister Campbell announced an election date. However, since both parties knew an election was coming, the campaign really began as soon as Campbell was elected as leader. From that outset, she had a number of disadvantages. The obvious one was that there was resentment in the Charest camp after Campbell defeated Charest to become party leader. The bitterness was especially pronounced in Quebec, where the Tories supporting Campbell and those who had supported Charest never really reached rapprochement. In conjunction with this direct bitterness were comments from Albertan Joe Clark (who had supported Charest) that Campbell was still a "stranger" to the party, comments that reminded Campbell of ones made during the previous campaign that had insistently called her a "rookie MP," despite her years of service and the fact that she had more cabinet experience upon becoming prime minister than ten of the eighteen men who had preceded her. The two less obvious disadvantages were the campaign team Campbell was saddled with and everyone's insistence on linking Campbell to Mulroney. And these disadvantages are connected, for the campaign team was Mulroney's. He insisted they were the best there was. Never having run a national parliamentary campaign, Campbell did not have either the wisdom to reject them or a strong alternative to suggest. The team could not—would not—escape the long shadow of the former prime minister. They treated Campbell as if she were Mulroney—keeping vehicles and rooms at the cool temperature he had preferred; they kept insisting that she consult Mulroney; and they backed away from any campaign strategy that might be conceived by anyone as critical of Mulroney. An objective analysis of the campaign would have suggested Campbell's need to distance herself from the former prime minister. The campaign team would not allow it. It is not then surprising that neither the media nor the public would either.

The media's unwillingness to forget Mulroney is perhaps best revealed when Campbell was speaking at a rally in Repentigny, Quebec. In response to the strong support there for a separatist third party, she remarked in French, "N'acceptez jamais d'etre deuxieme dans le pays que vous avez fonde" ("Never accept being second place in the country that you founded"). The comment was perfect. The press, however, in reporting it, argued, with no evidence at all, that Mulroney had given her the line to use. The public's unwillingness is perhaps best revealed when the *Globe and Mail* ran a series of stories suggesting the existence of a secret Conservative Party plan to cut social services that had been leaked to the newspaper. What the *Globe and Mail* had acquired was a draft proposal by some ministers that the party planned to offer for public comments along with other draft proposals after the election. It was not, as Campbell strongly stated, a secret plan. But the public believed it was because saying one thing but planning the opposite in secret was how they had come to think of Mulroney as operating. Similarly, the public—fueled by the liberal campaign—held a renovation project at Toronto's Lester Pearson International Airport against Campbell. Although the project was totally beyond reproach, the public believed insinuations of

Tory corruption under Campbell because they were convinced there had been Tory corruption under Mulroney.

Despite these disadvantages, Campbell gained high approval ratings from the public during her initial period of service as prime minister (although the party's numbers lagged behind). And during this period, media coverage changed its tone once again. Coverage turned positive once again: her early successes and energy made for a good story. The honeymoon, however, did not last long.

Late in the campaign, Vancouver radio personality Rafe Majr subjected her to selected call-ins (curiously all male) who attacked her policies and the fact that she had had two divorces. Slightly earlier, Toronto media personality Keith Morrison greeted the prime minister after a program by slapping her on the back and saying, "Great to see you, Kim," clearly not showing her any respect. The next day, she was harassed at a press scrum by media personality Hugh Winsor who, having finally provoked what he could claim was a gaffe, proceeded to argue to his media colleagues that they could use it to "crucify her." And the next day, when Campbell took a day off to deal with a bad cold, the media reported that she was off on a romantic weekend with boyfriend Gregory.

Some of this media coverage is simply "gotcha journalism" that might victimize a candidate whether male or female. Some of it may well be the media's revenge against the Conservative Party because it was offering fewer perks to the reporters on its bus than the liberals were on theirs. However, there is a distinctly gendered edge to the media behavior. Would the media have highlighted the personal life of a male political figure the way they did details of Campbell's? Would the media greeted Mulroney in the television studio with "Great to see you, Brian" the way they did Campbell?

And there is the question of fairness. Campbell did make comments she probably should not have made, such as telling *Toronto Sun* reporter Robert Fife to get a hearing aid when he asked her when she would offer policy positions immediately after she had just spent several minutes doing precisely that. Other times, however, her comments were clearly twisted into gaffes. For example, after announcing the election date, she entertained repeated questions on when the conservatives would reduce unemployment. She realistically suggested that the process would take years—into the latter half of the 1990s. Her comment was reported to be "not until the next century," and media figures then debated—gleefully—whether her comment was a new kind of political honesty or a major political gaffe. But the supposed gaffe was something she did not say. For another example, the gaffe that Winsor wanted to use to "crucify her" was an out-of-context remark. She meant to say that the brief, heated period of a parliamentary campaign was not the time to have an intricately detailed discussion of a policy matter; out of context, she seemed to say that campaigning was not the time for serious discussions. After some debate among media figures about whether to "crucify her" or not, the media declared this gaffe a defining moment in the campaign and then proceeded to make it such by covering it relentlessly. Liberal leader Jean Chretien said much the same thing two weeks later when asked for policy specifics. Curiously, his comments did not receive much coverage and certainly were not treated as—made into—a defining moment.

In analyzing media coverage of the parliamentary election, one is hard-pressed to separate out cleanly "gotcha journalism," a liberal bias, and sexism. Media commentators in Canada during and after the election drew attention to the latter two. Besides coverage of her personal life and a level of first-name familiarity one simply would not have presumed with a male prime minister, there was coverage focused on Campbell's personal appearance—her clothing and her weight. There was simply nothing comparable for Chretien. One might say that this was a courtesy because reporters did not want to draw attention to his disfigurement resulting from Bell's palsy during his youth. But why was the media so courteous toward Chretien and not toward Campbell?

The bias was perhaps most starkly clear in media coverage of the two debates (or policy forums) the candidates held, one in English and one in French. Immediate polling and focus groups showed Campbell triumphant in the English debate, despite the difficulties still posed by a format that put several candidates on stage and thereby limited direct, immediate responses. The media, however, helped along by very effective liberal party spinners, transformed a Campbell victory into a Campbell defeat. Interestingly, headlines focused on her defeat, not Chretien's victory. After the French language debate, the French press was highly flattering toward Campbell, complimenting her (remember: she's from "The West") command of French. The English press, on the other hand, faulted her French, claiming that the nonverbals that accompanied her searching her mind for a word made her look unstable.

The media probably did not by itself lead to the Tories' defeat in October 1993, but the media coverage, along with shrewd liberal attacks, played a major role. So did a poor Tory campaign. Not only was the Tory team poor in ways already discussed, it put Campbell almost constantly on the road. She did not get to know key campaign personnel, and they did not get to know her. She was not able to participate fully in the development of policy positions, resulting in one key interview where she misspoke (and quickly corrected herself) because she had just been handed *her* position. Her speeches were delivered to her too late for her to master, she was not allowed time to exercise or rest, and—as she found out gradually—the women who had so wanted to work on her campaign were largely frozen out of it by the largely male team the party imposed on her. Women were pushed out of the way, and incompetent men, such as the Edmonton party official who introduced her to speak on the Canadian economy by reviewing at length her marital difficulties, were put center stage.

Midway in the campaign, the tension surfaced over the issue of EH 101 helicopters. As defense minister, she strongly supported their purchase, and she had said so repeatedly. But her campaign people told her she had to back-off on that promise as a deficit-reduction gesture. She refused to cancel the purchase; eventually and reluctantly, she agreed to reduce it. When she announced that in a campaign speech, she came across as, just like Mulroney, a politician who pledged one thing but, then, delivered another. She was unhappy she had not stuck to her original position; the campaign team was unhappy she had balked at canceling the deal altogether.

Then, near the campaign's disastrous end, her team announced that it would run negative ads against Chretien. She was not shown them but was told about them by her team's leaders. Then, she found herself on an early morning news program being interviewed in French (she had been told the interview would be in English) and asked to defend the ads. She repeated what she had been told. When she finally saw the ads, she was livid and ordered them canceled immediately. She and her team's leaders "played chicken," and she won, but they did not suffer the public humiliation of having to renounce them and apologize for them.

The campaign team also kept her out of British Columbia. The team claimed that she needed to campaign heavily in Ontario and Quebec, not her home province. That neglect kept her from campaigning in her own riding in Vancouver. That lack of campaigning and the furor over the ads cost Campbell her own parliamentary seat. She would not only not be prime minister, she would also not be party leader of what was, after the election, a very minority party.

CONCLUSION

Anyone who studies election will tell you that they are not "neat." It is almost always impossible to say that factor *a* led to defeat or even that factors *a* and *b* led there. Richard Nixon's poor appearance in his initial debate against John F. Kennedy did not cause his defeat in 1960; neither did Gerald Ford's supposed gaffe about Soviet domination in eastern Europe in his debate against Jimmy Carter cause Ford's loss in 1976. Yes, both debate events undoubtedly contributed, but they were not the cause. They were mixed in with many, many other factors such as the Kennedy charisma and the Ford pardon of Nixon. Such is the case with the two campaigns examined in this chapter.

It would be easy—too easy—to say that Kim Campbell almost lost her campaign to be leader of the Conservative Party and, thereby, prime minister because of the sexism of the media and certain male political leaders. That was undoubtedly a factor, but so were other media attitudes. So was an awkward debate format that compelled her to either not respond to attacks or be perceived as overly aggressive if she did so. So did events in Somalia that made her, as defense minister, look bad, although neither what occurred in Africa nor her reserve in commenting should have been in any way to her discredit.

The parliamentary campaign is perhaps more complex. Much in the behavior of the media can be criticized. Reporters should not be trying to "crucify" candidates, regardless of party or gender; nor should they be spreading rumors about romantic weekends without any evidence whatsoever. They should not be so much into playing the campaign game themselves that they start creating gaffes and declaring them defining moments rather than covering the issues—genuine issues—raised during the campaign. Out-of-control, sometimes sexist, sometimes politically biased media were not, however, the reason the Tories went down in flames in 1993. They had a difficult time escaping the shadow of an unpopular Brian Mulroney, and—unbelievably—they did not even try that hard to do so by embracing the new elements Kim Campbell did bring to the party. They should have noted that, months into her ministry, her popularity was high while the party's was low. They should have hitched the campaign wagon to what Campbell brought to the party instead of to its party past. They ran a horrible campaign, and Campbell, although a victim of it, did not possess sufficient political savvy to ditch her advisors and find better ones (although a week before the campaign's end, she almost did just that).

So, is the story for women in politics much the same below and above the forty-eighth parallel? The answer is largely yes. Despite different political systems and elections that look similar but are strikingly different in how they work, sexist media coverage, cultural prejudices, biased political figures, and a glass ceiling all seem as Canadian as they do American. That Canada has had a female prime minister and the United States has not had a female president should not mislead us. Kim Campbell, arguably, slipped into the high office by being elected party leader of the majority party controlling the government. This is not the same as being nominated by a party for the presidency in the United States; this is certainly not the same being elected president in a November vote. Kim Campbell then lost that high office by not proving able to lead her party to a sufficient number of victories in parliamentary ridings scattered all across Canada. This loss is also not equivalent to losing the U.S. presidency. The situations are sufficiently different that, if one focuses just on elections *qua* elections—that is, events when people campaign and then people vote, one risks comparing apples, oranges, grapes, and peaches. What one needs to look at are the dynamics of the campaigns as this chapter has done. When one does that, the differences between the two national political traditions blur. Reporters look for gaffes, debates have troubling formats and then are spun, opponents toss out political red herrings, media figures excuse comments by men that they try to crucify women for, egos often get in the way of conducting the best campaign and selecting the best candidates and policies. These are political realities in Canada as well as in the United States, and, at least for the moment, women in both nations seem disadvantaged still by these and other realities.

NOTES

1. For example, see my edited collection, *Cracked But Not Shattered*, and Nichola Gutgold's *Almost Madam President*. Both books study the 2008 Hillary Clinton campaign, noting the many ways in which gender—but not gender alone—was an issue in that unsuccessful race. See also the study Nichola Gutgold, Diana Carlin, and I undertook of women who ought to have been considered for the presidency but were not, *Gender and the American Presidency*. We try, especially in the book's concluding chapter, to highlight the gendered barriers that exist to high office.

2. The Canadian culture values turn-taking and standing in line much more than the U.S. culture does.

3. The most useful study here is Kathleen Hall Jamieson's *Beyond the Double Bind*. In it, she presents several double-binds female candidates often find themselves in. These will be referred to a several points in this chapter. Also useful is the study of gendered campaigns undertaken by Dianne Bystrom, Mary Banwart, Lynda Lee Kaid, and Terry Robertson.

4. Biographical information on Campbell is derived largely from her memoirs, since her brief time in office has not inspired the biographical "industry" that Trudeau's years have.

5. Quoted in Campbell.

6. Quoted in Campbell.

THREE

Michael Manley's Rhetorical Consistency

Between 1955 and 1965, what had once been the British Empire gradually became a still-connected alliance of independent nations. Among these was the island nation of Jamaica. Its history prior to independence featured piracy, the slave trade, large plantations, and—then—a transitional time during which plantations went to ruinate, Kingston exploded into a large metropolitan area with urban problems reflecting first-world and third-world conditions, bauxite mining became a major and polluting industry, and skin color persisted as a line dividing not just white from black but not-as-black from more so. Upon independence, then, Jamaica had problems it had to face. While it advertised its beautiful north coast beaches to tourists, it had to deal with issues that, for the most part, originated elsewhere on the island.

Many nations that became independent from Great Britain have political histories that are mind-boggling with many government changes and many political personalities. Jamaica's, on the other hand, is simple. It has two political parties, the Jamaican Labor Party (JLA) and the People's National Party (PNP); and, since independence, it has alternated between the two JLA-PNP-JLA-PNP with the dominant PNP leader clearly being Michael Manley. He was initially opposition leader; then, he was PNP prime minister. Then, opposition leader again until the PLP expressed its displeasure with the JLA government by withdrawing totally from government. Then, PNP prime minister again until his retirement. For a quarter of a century, Michael Manley was the PNP.

In between Michael Manley's first stint and his second, the prime minister was JLP leader Edward Seaga. Seaga was, unlike his predecessor Manley, who was open to communist leaders and therefore not on good terms with the United States, was America's Caribbean friend. More im-

portant, Seaga believed in market forces. He led Jamaica away from Manley's "democratic socialism" that featured attempts to provide a high
level of government services along with considerable government regula-
tion of economic activity. The time of Seaga's government was a tense
time: urban discontent rose, as did violence and drug dealing. The poor
felt that his policies did not have that segment of the island's population
in view. Thus, eventually, the PNP regained power. When it did, Manley
had changed his view on how Jamaica needed to proceed as an economic
entity. Put bluntly, he felt that Seaga's focus on market forces and the
private sector was largely correct. So, although he was returned to the
prime minister's office to reverse Seaga's policies, he wanted to continue
them.[1]

Manley very much believed in communication. Whether in or out of
power, he spoke, and he spoke at length. He spoke before the legislature;
he spoke on television. Communication, then, was his way of sharing his
vision. Returning to power, he could have told the people that his vision
had changed, but he did not. Although he did suggest that one's politics
evolve and that those in public service necessarily learn from experience
and adapt their approaches, he tried to present a consistent picture of
himself and the PNP. So, although he was a socialist who favored big
government the first time but a capitalist who believed the private sector
had an important role to play in the nation the second, he tried to be the
same man. This chapter will suggest that Manley largely succeeded in a
difficult rhetorical task—convincing the people that he was the same man
even though he was cozy with Fidel Castro during his first term and
good buddies with George H. W. Bush during his second.

The chapter will consider five of Manley's speeches, pointing to the
rhetorical elements that allowed him to bridge this gap. The speeches
were selected to span Manley's career. The first was delivered on July 7,
1991, while Manley was leader of the opposition; the second, from July
26, 1972, occurred just after Manley took the reins of government. The
third, dated May 27, 1975, finds Manley well into his initial term as prime
minister; the fourth—May 22, 1980—is from later in his initial ministry.
The last, dated May 22, 1991, is from his second term. All five are parliamentary addresses, and, whether they are opposition addresses or prime
minister's addresses, they have the feel of an American State of the Union
Address insofar as they survey what is going on in the nation's domestic
and (less so) foreign affairs. They are all quite lengthy: evidently Jamaican members of Parliament have the patience to sit through speeches
that, at times, are quite prosaic as they explore education, agriculture,
crime, the International Monetary Fund, and the lottery. The latter four
addresses seem to cover most of the topics relevant to governance; the
first, given from the opposition point-of-view, does seem to focus just a
bit more on just those topics that impact the poorer people of the island.
This difference is what one would expect: although they all resemble

State of the Union addresses, the first is from an opposition point-of-view and thus more attentive to the concerns of the group that is most clamoring for a change in government.

The perorations also reflect where in "the story" we are. In 1971, Manley says he has a dream and a plan and offers the PNP's pledges to the people in the upcoming election. In 1972, after assuming power, he calls for hard work to reach the goals the PLP has set for the nation. In 1975, Manley's radical voice is apparent in his call for a peaceful revolution as he and his government move gradually toward the national goals the PNP has set. Implicit is his awareness that the goals are proving more difficult to reach than had been expected and that there is some discontent. He keeps alive the desire for revolution on the part of the more oppressed people but insist on its being peaceful. And in 1980, near an election, he concludes by highlighting the choices the people need to make between the PNP and JLP. This parliamentary address sounds more like a campaign speech than a State of the Union. Finally, in 1991, back in power after years in opposition, he echoes an earlier PNP theme by calling for putting people first. His rhetorical need to recall this PNP slogan in 1991 will be discussed later.

What is interesting in the five addresses are the sections that we might term "philosophical," sections in which Manley puts the particulars of government behind and talks about his vision for the country and his philosophy of governing. These sections are "Need for Vision" in 1971; "Change Must Come" in 1972; "Democratic Socialism" in 1975; both "Communism" and "Differences between the PNP and JLP" in 1980; and both a section entitled "Mood in the Country," which leads to a decade by decade survey of the country's policies, and a section entitled (again) "Democratic Socialism" in 1991. "Putting People First," this last speech's peroration, is also part of this last speech's philosophical discussion. The fact that he needed to say more about governmental philosophy in 1991 is revealing, for the exigence in 1991 is the feeling by many that the new Manley is not the same as the old. He therefore needs to present his philosophy at length to demonstrate its consistency despite certain changes in policies.

Three clusters of ideas are to be found in all five of these addresses — in these philosophical sections. They arguably give the speeches — and Michael Manley — the consistency he desires. The first centers on the people. He wants the people — all of the people — to both have power and have their economic needs attended to. The second centers on the entwined notes of equality and justice, for in Manley's rhetoric, equality is prerequisite to justice. The third centers on dynamism. Jamaica is, in his view, a nation creating itself. It is trying to move forward; it is trying to progress. The process will not always prove easy, but the process — and the progress — must be in view. Manley's rhetoric will attain a consistency to the extent he is able to keep these clusters alive in his speeches.

JULY 1971

In this address, Manley declares that, "We must remember that the essence of democracy is people controlling power."[2] As he surveys the Jamaican political situation from his position as leader of the opposition, he suggests that power has "more and more tend[ed] to fall into the hands of a few political leaders." He is, of course, indicting the JLP government. He notes that "Once in power, the politicians [i.e., the JLP politicians] have become more and more concerned with holding power than with the upholding of principle." He sees their concern with holding power in how they have manipulated both parliamentary ridings through gerrymandering and the constitution of the voting electorate by registration procedures that disadvantage the poor.

Manley believes the people should have the power, and he believes that the government should help the people. The JLP government is, in his view, "ignoring the essential pre-conditions of progress, that is the development of the human resources, the development of the human-being." People are "without jobs" and therefore they have "no hope and no economic protection." He argues that the JLP keeps detailed data on trivial matters such as how many tins of corned beef are available but exhibits its contempt for the poor by maintaining no specific data on how many are impoverished on the island.

The Jamaican people must have, Manley declares, "equal access to the law." They must also have equal access to opportunities. And the routes to the economic equality are "through our education," "[t]hrough access to the political system," [t]hrough access to the institutions of Government," and "[t]hrough access to the economic system which means not only jobs but a chance to play a part, a creative and constructive part[,] in the workings of the system." Only when there is the equality—legal and economic—will Jamaica be "a society worthy of the term 'social justice.'"

Jamaica is, Manley insists, a country his listeners "are trying to build," "are trying to create." He talks in terms of the nation's vision, the nation's dream. There is, in the address, a sense of forward progress begun before independence and pushed onward by independence that has now been thwarted by the JLP of government of Hugh Shearer. Manley wants the movement to resume.

Manley in 1971 clearly focuses on the people, their need for power and equality. He also sounds a dynamic note of potential progress if the forces that are thwarting it can be surmounted by a change in government from JLP to PNP.

JULY 1972

The same three themes of the people, equality and justice, and dynamic movement are found a year later after a PNP victory and after Manley becomes Prime Minister.

Manley is still, to some extent, looking back to the JLP government, for he indicts those who "value things above people." He tells his audience that "the person . . . is more important" and that "things only exist to the extent that they can serve the people." Putting people first means, in Manley's view, that the accumulation of material goods—many of them luxuries—needs to cease. Instead, the focus must be on those items the people need—employment, housing, and nutrition. He tells his auditors that, "no other right has any meaning unless a man has food, clothing, and shelter."

If the people have these basic needs addressed, then there can be "a society of equality, a society of social justice." In Manley's view, equality and social justice are intertwined, but neither is truly possible unless basic needs are addressed. It is government's role to ensure that those basic needs are indeed addressed.

He tells his listeners—and in this address, he seems to be speaking to more than just the fellow members of the legislature—that the Jamaican people need to know "where we want to go," "where we are trying to get." Dynamism is incipient in this call, but does not exist unless the people commit to a vision for the country. Perhaps Manley's shift from opposition to government is evident in his declaration that, "progress depends first of all on a force that comes from inside a man." He notes that, "Nobody can legislate for progress from outside if a man does not have the will to acquire progress for himself." So, government alone is not the answer: the people must work to push themselves and their nation forward.

MAY 1975

The Manley PNP government is well underway by now, and this address reflects that fact. It is a very long speech, and it discusses practically every matter of government that one might think of, including whether or not Jamaica should or should not be the site of a beauty pageant. The level of detail far surpasses anything one might find in a U.S. State of the Union address. This mass of detail does not, however, prevent Manley from offering comments that are more philosophical. In fact, at this time in his first government, he is at his most philosophical—both here and in written texts. He had begun to term his approach to government "Democratic Socialism," and he discusses what he means by the term in the most philosophical section of this lengthy 1975 address.

Undoubtedly displeasing certain auditors abroad, Manley declares, "We are a Socialist Government." He quickly defines what he means: "The final aim of socialism is the creation of a just society based on the principle of equality, self-reliance, discipline and participation by all of the people in the process of Government and the running of the economy." Implicit in this statement of governmental purpose are Manley's three recurring themes. Socialism does not involve a dictator; rather, the people. They are involved in the government, and they are involved in the economy.

The shared goal of the government and the people involves equality and social justice. These intertwined values are still at the core of Manley's thinking. To achieve them, dynamic action is necessary. The people must participate, and the government's role becomes mobilization. The government must create an environment that foments action and, then, push those who are reluctant to get involved in it to get involved. A Manley government will prevent those at the low end of the socioeconomic ladder from being exploited; however, a Manley government will be just as intolerant of indigence as of exploitation.

Manley entitled this lengthy speech "Embracing Democratic Socialism." His vision—version one—is at its peak, and the speech seems fairly optimistic about achieving that vision's goals. There are many policy particulars—both foreign and domestic—that need to be addressed, but if the government does its part and the people do theirs, Jamaica has a bright future. It is important, however, to contextualize this address in the global economy. It's 1975, and the economic boom of the 1960s is over. Inflation and unemployment exist together—in defiance of traditional economic theory—posing problems in many nations, and oil prices are soaring and oil supplies are dwindling. Manley's optimism may soon run into sour economic realities that transcend Jamaica.

MAY 1980

This address is defensive, for the Manley government has been challenged by the JLP on a number of fronts. Manley's response is quite vigorous, but, between the lines, is the message that there are forces that, try as he might, Manley cannot control. He can point to achievements; he acknowledges shortcomings. He frequently notes the difficulties facing the nation. He does not, however, retreat from his fundamental beliefs in the people, in equality and social justice, and in progress.

As one might expect, however, he does not want to admit that the continuing problems in Jamaica are either ones he cannot solve because his policies are inappropriate or because they are so large (so global) as to be beyond his reach. So, he spends time in the address blaming those (primarily the JLP opposition) who are preventing the PNP from achieving its goals. Thus, the section in the 1980 address labeled "Communism," in which Manley talks about how opponents have used the insinuation that his government is Communist to thwart its proposals.

Manley first establishes that the PNP, as a democratic entity, has established repeatedly what it is and that it remains committed to democratic socialism. The PNP's position can be found in many party documents, Manley insists: it is not a secret. If one were to examine the PNP record, one would find "total respect for a plural democracy" that most definitely involved the private sector. The PNP has, Manley makes clear, believed in "total rights of the private businessman, total rights of the private sector." The problem is that others—the JLP opposition primarily—have labeled the PNP as "Communist" and have created an impression that the PNP government will be likely to confiscate property. Hysteria has resulted, and this hysteria has resulted in the lack of economic growth in the island nation. As Manley says, "The reason why Jamaica is still experiencing negative growth is because in that condition of hysteria, largely induced by certain elements in the Opposition seeing the opportunity to keep the economy constantly off balance." He points to "eight and a quarter years in office with total respect for the private sector." He notes that "nobody [has] expropriated anybody's property, stole anybody's rights." He insists on a balance between the private sector and the state.

This lengthy discussion of private interests and the state is interesting in itself, but it will prove more interesting when in the second Manley government, the Prime Minister is portrayed as shifting radically from state-based socialism to a reliance on the private sector and market forces. The 1980 speech suggests that Manley's position was already nuanced. Yet he is portrayed by media differently. And, in the 1980 address, he criticizes the Jamaican media for presenting his government's position in terms that feed the hysteria and the international media for picking up on the story of a Communist-leaning Jamaica and scaring away foreign business interests. He points to a story in an American newspaper "that there were 5,000 Cuban soldiers in the Jamaican Army." He laughs it off, noting that the total Jamaican army is only three thousand, but does speak out strongly against the message being sent that Jamaica does not believe in and respect the rights of the private sector.

So, Manley does not acknowledge completely his government's responsibility for the nation's continuing economic difficulties: he tries to place some blame on the Opposition JLP and on the media. He does not back off from the principles that the PNP had long espoused; however, he tries to clarify the role that the private sector played in the PNP vision.

At the end of the address, he does offer that vision. The same hallmarks of the people, equality and justice, and progress are still present. However, what is strikingly different in this peroration is how Manley internationalizes the vision. After again noting the PNP's "mutual respect

for the private sector," he rejects the obsession of others with the Cold
War and an East-West view of international affairs. He says the PNP does
not believe that, "the issues of the Cold War are really of fundamental
concern to the poor of the world." What is of interest are the North-South
issues, for they relate to the "economic justice of the world." He stresses
the needs of the Jamaican people, especially their need for equality across
class lines and economic justice, but in a context he terms "unapologeti-
cally internationalist."

Manley also stresses how the people of Jamaica must work to meet
their goals. "Jamaicans must constantly work . . . to build economic independence." The role of government is to plan and to direct this dynamic
movement forward. Manley entitles this peroration the "Difference Between PNP and JLP," so he very much sees a campaign ahead. Read as a
campaign call, the peroration then both declares principles and defends
against likely challenges. The declaration is largely unchanged from the
rhetoric we have seen thus far—the people, equality and justice, and
progress. The defense had Manley insisting that he is not opposed to the
private sector and, in fact, embraces it in his vision for a prosperous
nation. The defense also had him saying that Jamaica's quest not only
necessitates an involvement in global affairs but an involvement along
lines that make the accusation that he is a communist irrelevant.

MAY 1991

The PNP will lose the election. The JLP government headed by Seaga will
take office and push the nation in more of a market economy direction
and toward a strikingly pro-Western foreign policy. Manley heads an
opposition PNP. Then, with tensions increasing, the PNP will pull out of
the government entirely in protest of a direction that the PNP believes
oppresses the poor. Eventually, the PNP reengages and, then, wins a
majority in the legislature. Manley forms his second government.

His May 1991 address is a fairly early one in this second government,
but, even though early, it was delivered far enough into his government
that it was clear that he was taking a somewhat different direction when
it came to building the nation. He was not surprisingly criticized, so this
speech becomes his opportunity to explain how his new position is consistent with the principles that have governed the PNP since its begin-
nings.

Manley turns teacher—a history teacher—to accomplish this rhetorical goal. He begins with the late colonial period during which, despite the
people's characteristic independence, they were trapped in an economy
that was controlled by either the colonial power or a small number of
Jamaicans who were more loyal to the crown than to the people. The
result was an economy that he repeatedly calls "warped." It was, in his

view, warped in a manner that favored the privileged, not the people at large.

Manley then considers the 1960s, the initial decade of independence. It was, he acknowledges, a time of "very substantial growth." The growth, however, was totally economic; the social situation—rife with inequalities—was largely unchanged. Furthermore, the growth was not directed: in a sense, it just happened. There was a booming bauxite-mining industry; there was a booming hotel and tourism industry. Viewed from the outside, Jamaica seemed prosperous but a closer examination would have revealed considerable stagnation and, as a result, popular unrest.

He then turns to the 1970s during which his PNP government addressed the socioeconomic inequalities in the nation by state action. He now terms this "an error, a mistake." Yes, he argues, "whole generations of poor people . . . for the first time knew opportunities"; however, the economy as a whole was "not really strong enough" to support his PNP's "great emphasis on income redistribution." If the state-focus of economic planning was an error, the goal of income redistribution was not so much erroneous as premature .

Manley critiques the 1980s by rather surprisingly arguing that it was a mistake to embrace timidly the market economy. His government was timid, but so—he suggests—was the Seaga government. The real problem was the Seaga government's belief that economic development through participation in a market economy would solve all of the nation's difficulties. An emphasis on a market economy—Manley is suggesting—needed to be coupled with a concern for the people and the entwined issues of equality and justice. The 1980s, Manley argues, "showed at times a quite catastrophic social reversal." Those people Manley and the PNP were concerned for moved backward not forward under JLP leadership. The private sector, then, at the heart of the market economy approach needed to be pushed more by the government and it needed to be pushed in a direction that served the nation's impoverished people who did not feel equal and did not believe they were being treated justly.

Manley's principles, it should be noted, have remained the same. What he accomplishes in this address so far is to shift the debate between a state-directed economy and a market-directed economy from a debate over fundamentals to a debate over means. The debate, then, becomes trivial in the sense that it does not affect, either way, the fundamental message Manley is delivering.

Finally, Manley talks about the 1990s. In this section, he establishes the primary goal the nation must focus on if it is to achieve the overarching goals of the PNP. The country must, Manley tells its legislative leaders (and others), "solve the problem of production." He says, "We must get the production, traditional production, new production, production in services, production in tourism, production in everything." This rhetorical flourish certainly sounds more capitalist than socialist, and it leads Manley to again talk about the presumed means to production, the private sector.

Manley admits that one of the PNP's problems with the private sector is that it is "seen . . . as carrying a certain kind of specific class connotation." Without denying the truth of this perception, he tries to redefine the private sector somewhat by noting that, "The private sector is not just the big corporations and the old signs of the plutocracy, whatever you call it. The private sector is everybody who is in there with some spirit of business sense that we call entrepreneurship, big and small, major and micro." Having then embraced the private sector as a means to its unchanged goals, Manley tries to make the private sector more palatable to those who had embraced a socialist message that stressed state action over private sector action driven by marketplace forces.

An inevitable question given Manley's shift here concerns the "democratic socialism" he had earlier proclaimed. Thus, there is a section in the address labeled "Democratic Socialism," in which Manley would address the question head-on. He knows that he has auditors who want to know if "it [his more market oriented approach] is consistent with what they call principles of democratic socialism." He answers the question in two ways. First, he argues that ideologies are inherently "evolving" and therefore that "some of the older articles of faith have proved to be wanting" as time has proceeded. The dominance of state action is evidently one of those. However, Manley wants to make it clear that—and this is his second answer—"democratic socialism never based its objectives, its purposes on the idea of state action in the economy." Democratic socialism was all about using political action "to achieve equality of opportunity in a society . . . to underwrite and guarantee social justice in a society." He then adds that "only a simpleton or a propagandist . . . really thinks that the purpose of it was about state control." Notice again that Manley tries to sustain the principles of his PNP government while suggesting that the means may have changed somewhat from state action to private sector action.

But Manley even refuses to admit fully this change. He tells his audience that "no PNP manifesto in history, no democratic socialist manifesto in history has ever failed to say that they believe in at least the mixed economy, have faith in the positive and dynamic role of a private sector within that economy." If one looks at PNP initiatives "to encourage the private sector . . . the inclusion of private sector dynamic [within the PNP ideology] cannot be questioned."

Well, undoubtedly many do indeed question it, but, even if we grant that Manley's positions are not entirely consistent throughout his career, we still need to consider whether he manages in his rhetoric to project sufficient consistency. This chapter's argument has been that he does. He does so by stressing certain fundamental principles—the people, their right to equality and social justice, and the nation's (sometimes slow) progress. The means to these goals may indeed have shifted—more or less so depending on how persuasive one finds Manley, but the means emerge in his rhetoric as secondary to the goals. Early, goals and means may well have been conflated somewhat. If Manley's rhetoric is deft, it is so in his ability to separate the means from the goals and to then argue that, although the shift in the means has not been as dramatic as some might claim, the goals have remained unflinchingly the same throughout his political career.

NOTES

1. A good discussion of Manley's progression in economic policy is David Panton's *Jamaica's Michael Manley: The Great Transformation (1972–1992)* (Kingston: LMH Publishing, 1993).

2. Manley's speeches are quoted from Delano Franklyn's *Michael Manley: The Politics of Equality* (Kingston: Delano Franklyn, 2012).

FOUR

Bob Marley's Rhetorical Journey to Pan-Africanism

In Kingston, Jamaica, there stands a statue memorializing one of the nation's greatest heroes, Bob Marley. Yes, music is important; and it certainly has been important in Jamaica where a succession of styles such as ska, rock-steady, reggae, and raga have played a role in the global evolution of popular music.[1] But "rock stars," even though prominent, are rarely given a national place of honor in the manner Marley is in Jamaica.

Perhaps the reason is that Marley was more than a "rock star." He was an important political figure as well—not because he ran for or served in public office (which he did not), but because he communicated important political messages.

Music and politics often coincide. In the United States, the corporate forces controlling popular music in the 1950s did their best to keep anything controversial out of the product they were—for the most part—asking young artists to perform. But, at the same time, folk music, which was growing in popularity in Greenwich Village, in Newport, and on college campuses, was raising political issues. The "folk-rock" genre popular in the late 1960s and early 1970s brought the political into even more and farther-reaching popular music.

Marley's progression as an artist is somewhat parallel—from music that sounded common, politically innocuous themes to music that offered political observations. Why popular music—in the case of the United States as well as in the case of Bob Marley—followed this trajectory is difficult to ascertain. The best explanation may well be that certain issues became so important—and, thanks to the media, so prominent, that artists felt they had to engage them. In the United States, those issues were brought to the fore by a succession of social movements that crusaded against injustice and war. In Jamaica, issues—not exactly the same ones—were brought to the fore by the PNP.

Before Jamaica's independence, the PNP focused its attention on the island's impoverished people, and its rhetoric noted that the wealth in Jamaica was distributed along racial lines. After independence, this message became more intense. And those in the slums of Kingston heard it. Marley was born in rural Jamaica, but, at age twelve, he moved to the Kingston slum of Trench Town.[2] There, in the 1960s, he turned to music. Gradually, his music acquired a political edge, and this edge associated him in most people's minds with the PNP. He was always primarily a musician, but the attempt in 1976 to assassinate him suggests that he was seen by many in political, not musical, terms.

The mid to late 1970s were a tense period in Jamaican political history. The JLP had replaced the PNP at the head of the government, and the PNP had progressed through a period of disengagement followed by violent election campaigns. Perhaps the pinnacle of Marley's political activity was his bringing PNP leader Michael Manley and JLP leader Edward Seaga to the stage together at the "One Love" concert in 1978. The speech act was Marley's way of saying that Jamaica, especially its needy people, were more important than either Manley's more socialist politics or Seaga's more free market politics. The concert called for "One Love," a commitment that might unite the battling politicians and parties in a peaceful effort to find the best ways to help Jamaica.

Marley died three years later, at age thirty-six, of cancer. After the "One Love" concert, he entered a period of decline. And, although political historians may well point to the concert as Marley's most important political act, his influence on the people of Jamaica was less through that one speech act and more through a succession of songs.

Marley's body of work as songwriter is huge. Others have studied it—as music and as poetry.[3] What I wish to do in this chapter is not to repeat the work of others who have, in many cases, delved deeply into some songs as one might a complex lyric poem but trace a progression in the songs. It is a political progression, and I wish to suggest that Marley wanted his auditors—in and out of Jamaica—to follow him along this progression.

The progression proceeds through eleven songs: "Trench Town," "Concrete Jungle," "No Woman No Cry," "Slave Driver," "Redemption Song," "Burnin' and Lootin'," "Rastaman Live Up," "Get Up, Stand Up," "War," "Africa Unite," and "Zimbabwe." These are not only some of Marley's most overtly political songs, but they are also some of his most well-known ones.

"TRENCH TOWN"

Trench Town is the poor section of Kingston Marley moved to at age twelve and grew up in. But in the song "Trench Town," Marley envisions the place not as a part of Jamaica's largest city but, rather, the Biblical Egypt in which the Israelites were held as slaves. He talks about his life in this place as being imprisoning but he can see that the oppression, which he presents figuratively as seas, leads to a promised land beyond, that promised land being the Jamaica that could be.

He promises to lead the people through the oppression to freedom with music—that is, with the political message he is delivering in his songs. Once beyond the oppression, the people will, like the Israelites, be in something akin to the Sinai Desert. But, there, they will find substance just as the Israelites found manna on the ground in the mornings. Those observing the people's progress will, then, see history repeating itself: just as Moses led his captive people out of Egypt, Marley will lead those imprisoned within the poverty of Trench Town out of deprivation.

This progress is, however, a vision, not a reality. Toward the song's end, Marley looks at the reality, making a number of astute observations concerning the government's communication as well as concerning justice.

Marley notes that, in general, the government's negative communication about the people of Trench Town makes the government feel stronger. The government, then, boosts its illusion of power by putting down the poor people of Kingston. Thus, when Marley further notes that the government says that nothing good comes out of Trench Town, this is then just an example of the government putting down the people and the put-down increasing the government's illusion of power, as is the label of "underprivileged people," which the government gives the poor in Trench Town. These put-downs enhance the government's illusion of power: communication is being used to enhance the illusion. This last time, however, the government chains the people with that illusion. In other words, because the people believe that they are "underprivileged," they become dependent on government action. This dependency chains them. Whether the government makes the people feel weak and dependent just to demonstrate its rhetorical power or out of fear for the masses is unclear. After all, if you fear a group because of its numbers, disempowering that group through rhetoric may well be a shrewd government strategy.

The people of Trench Town—by extension, the impoverished people of Jamaica—are not, however, portrayed as a threat by Marley. Rather, they are loving and giving—toward each other and toward the nation. Recognizing their benevolence, the government, Marley argues, has an obligation to repay it—both to reciprocate it and pay tribute to it.

"CONCRETE JUNGLE"

"Concrete Jungle" also presents Trench Town and similar urban places as a figurative prison lacking bars and other constraining devices but nonetheless denying freedom. Rather than use a Biblical analogy to depict the place, Marley uses the metaphor of darkness. No sun shines; no moon. Day has become night, and night has become still darker. As a result, the love and the life characteristic of the oppressed Jamaican people in "Trench Town" can no longer be seen.

What then should the people do? The song suggests that self-help is at least the beginning of a response, for the singer sings to himself that he has to get off the dirt floor. But the singer then suggests that self-help, although it might take one beyond the metaphorical "concrete jungle," will only lead to the illusion of freedom. The suggestion is that Jamaica as a whole, not just the slum, is imprisoning. The song then is somewhat confusing: it calls its listeners to act for freedom but, then, suggests that that action may not be enough to reach that goal. The song has an optimistic moment, but, then, a despairing one.

"NO WOMAN NO CRY"

This song similarly sits on the cusp between despair and optimism. Despair is the consequence of living in Trench Town, where not only are there hardships but there seem to be as many hypocrites as there are people who mean the good things they do and say. The singer tries to focus on the latter. They are the people who will share the firewood they have with the community; they are the people who will share the food they have with the community. Heartened by these beneficent people, the poet tells the woman not to cry; he tells her that everything will be fine. The poet, however, notes that his agency is limited, figuring his limitations by noting he has his feet for transportation but nothing else. He will nonetheless but slowly go somewhere; he will, thus, do something. In the interim, his message to the woman is to not shed any tears.

"SLAVE DRIVER"

In "Slave Driver," Marley makes a turn into history and a move toward greater activism. Whereas the history envisioned earlier was that of the Old Testament Jewish people, the history now is that of the African people. Before turning to history in the song, the singer makes it clear to the slave driver that the historical situation between slave driver and slave has been reversed. Fire is forecast, and the slave driver is the one who will be burned in this new flame.

The song then goes back in time to the cargo ships that transported slaves from Africa to the "New World." As any Jamaican knows, a major stop along the way was "Port Royal" along Jamaica's southern coast. This city, known for its roles in piracy and slavery, was destroyed in an earthquake, and many writers have suggested that its wickedness brought on God's destruction much in the manner of the Biblical Sodom and Gomorrah.

The song notes the literal enslavement on the ships. Then, it compares that enslavement to life now which claims to be a free one but is really just another kind of slavery, that of poverty. The song implies more, however. It implies that the government is deliberately keeping the poor people of Jamaica illiterate so that they will not be able to acquire the knowledge that would cause them to question their situation. The song also implies that the government is some kind of mechanical equipment designed to make money. The suggestion is that the capitalistic economy functions in such a manner that the poor remain poor and the rich can try to be oblivious. It is not the governing of people's policies that impoverish; no, it's just the way the economy functions and the way the markets works.

It is worth noting that PNP policy and Michael Manley's rhetoric took a pronounced Marxist turn at about the time "Slave Driver" was written. Marley's thoughts seem, then, to be evolving along a progression that matches that of the political party he was identified with.

"REDEMPTION SONG"

In this song, Marley blends the two histories he referred to in earlier songs. He envisions the lot of slaves, as merchandise, kept in their passages across the ocean in the pits of overcrowded ships in which many died. He pairs that story with that of the Biblical Israel, which saw various forces murder its prophets—including Jesus—and were then told that the deaths occurred to fulfill prophecy.

Besides slavery, the link is that both groups had their redemption songs. Slaves sang songs that seemed to look forward to glory in heaven but may have, between the songs' lines, preached revolution. The Jews, after Christ's death, turned Christians and sang new songs—that is, said Masses—that celebrated the grand redemption of Easter morning. As in "Trench Town," Marley points to music as the force that will lead the oppressed beyond oppression. In neither song is he literally pointing to music: music serves as a metaphor for the range of messages that might be sent. And, in "Redemption Song," it is no longer one person's music, for it has become a community's. Marley's song, in fact, tries to create that community by asking his auditors to join in these songs offering freedom.

"BURNIN' AND LOOTIN'"

Sometimes, however, words are not enough. "Burnin' and Lootin'" suggests that Jamaica has reached that point. However, it is worth noting that the song is really two songs in one, for it calls for violent action in the first and third choruses, but it anticipates the more passive suffering in the middle chorus.

The song figures the singer and the people as prisoners. Whereas before, the prison was largely in one's mind, reinforced by government attitudes, now, the prison seems more real. The fact that there is a government-imposed curfew makes the prison seem less purely metaphorical; the fact that looming over the singer were uniformed, brutal guards makes the prison seem less purely metaphorical. Marley also notes the presence of drugs and how they sap revolutionary energy, bringing in a very real note given the problems with drug trafficking that beset Kingston at the time. The prison of the song, then, floats somewhere between metaphorical and real and functions on both levels: it describes the people's situation, but there are more and more armed guards present to enforce the nightly curfew. As these guards become prominent, disturbing metaphor emerges into terrifying reality.

The song also recalls the situation of the Biblical Israelites as well as songs often sung by slaves. These talk about crossing rivers, be they real Jordans or figurative ones. Marley expresses some frustration with these rivers because there seems to be so many to cross and no sense of necessarily getting anywhere important on the next bank where someone important might be spoken to and that important person might listen. He suggests that those who are rioting and looting are not trying to reach the promised land of material wealth but, instead, the much more limited goal of a conversation about their plight with the prime minister or some other person with political influence. The song, then, is not a revolutionary anthem but, rather, a restrained plea born out of frustration. Nonetheless, the song does through its title and refrain forecast that there will be "Burnin' and a-lootin'" without passing any judgment on the violence. (One might suggest that the lilt of the reggae rhythm gives the observation something of a celebratory tone.)

"RASTAMAN LIVE UP"

"Rastaman Live Up" is ostensibly addressed to a number of politicized performers—in Jamaica and elsewhere in the Caribbean—who both speak out against the government and try to sustain island culture. "Bongoman" is a persona adopted by Jamaican reggae artist Jimmy Cliff; "Congoman," a persona adopted by Trinidad calypso artist "The Mighty Sparrow"; and "Rastaman," a persona used in early albums by the group of musicians Marley himself was associated with. Marley's message is "don't give up," despite what the government, figured as a predatory creature, might do.

To encourage his fellow artists, Marley uses Biblical allusions. They are like David, who, clearly the underdog, slew Goliath with just a sling-shot and a stone. They are like Samson, who, thought to be beaten, slew the Philistines by pulling down the pillars supporting their temple. If these performers persist, Marley says, there will come an Armageddon. Marley is probably not predicting a battle that announces the second coming; rather, he is predicting a battle that will herald the "end times" for a government that oppresses the people. After the battle, the govern-ment will fall into a kind of confusion just as people did after the Biblical Tower of Babel became disturbingly multilingual.

Is Marley calling for a literal battle? Has he changed from one who thought words could change the world to one who thinks violence will be necessary? The answer is difficult to discern from either Marley's lyr-ics or anything he did or said. The essential point to note is how Marley has clearly progressed over a rather short time period from a musician who speaks up to a musician who is militant.

"GET UP, STAND UP"

Marley had embraced the Rastafarian religion. With roots in Ethiopia, it was based in Judaism and Christianity, but it went far beyond these in granting divinity to Ethiopian ruler Haile Selassie and in its ritualistic use of cannabis. Among the reasons people in Jamaica turned to Rastafarian beliefs was what many felt was traditional Christianity's refusal to pro-vide much assistance to the nation's impoverished people. "Get Up, Stand Up" only reflects Rastafarian beliefs implicitly: we know Marley was a Rasta; therefore, we hear the song as a Rasta song. Without that biographical knowledge, we would probably just read the song as being opposed to traditional religion.

Traditional religion's focus on heavenly rewards is what Marley in-dicts. Preachers should not, Marley says, be telling poor people that they should be looking for the good life only on the other side of the grave. That message encourages waiting patiently for death or the second com-ing; it discourages questioning a status quo that features stark differences between rich and poor. Traditional religion is also criticized for spending too much time on the "technicalities" of theology, with new churches coming and going accordingly. Marley declares that these theological arguments deflect attention from the mission churches should be on— helping people. The song repeatedly encourages people—Rastas and non-Rastas alike—to not give up the cause of economic justice. What is stressed in the song is not to give up in the face of messages delivered from some pulpits, but the overall message in the song is simply not to give up. Marley was aware that religion was far from the only social force in Jamaica suppressing the people's will.

"WAR"

In "War," it is clear how violent a response Marley is now calling for. What is clear is that war is necessary in Marley's view until racism ends and human rights are available equally to all. Midway through the song, though, it seems as if Marley's focus changes. Although the first half of the song makes no direct references to Jamaica, it can be read as speaking about the racism Marley has discerned all around him in his native land. Midway through, he starts speaking about goals that are international: he calls for world peace and speaks about a world citizenship. Marley's concern as an artist is no longer just Jamaica.

What has pushed Marley in this direction is apparent in the song's next stanzas, in which he narrows his global focus to just Africa. He talks about politics in Angola, Mozambique, and South Africa. Regimes there, he tells a primarily Jamaican audience, hold those united with Jamaicans by the color of their skin in a kind of bondage. Now, the political particulars certainly differ from African nation to African nation, as well as from Africa to the Caribbean and beyond in the African diaspora. In "War," Marley is ignoring the differing particulars, for he is embracing the political cause of Africans no matter where and no matter the political particulars. In doing so, Marley is scarcely unique: many in the Caribbean and elsewhere were developing an identity as Africans first and residents in whatever state later at this time. The importance of Marley's embrace of the broader identity is that, as popular music performer in Jamaica and globally, he had the power to convey this message more persuasively and widely than many.

"AFRICA UNITE"

As the title of this song suggests, the African focus of "War" continues in "Africa Unite." Like the former song, it deals little with political particulars. Rather, it calls for a united Africa now that, figuratively, Africans are moving out of a Babylonian captivity and home to the promised land. Although Marley will call for unity under the banner of the Rastafarian religion, he uses an Old Testament analogy to tell his history. Babylon is slavery; the promised land, economic freedom, and economic justice. So, in Marley's vision, slavery in all of its guises is vanishing, and, with the long Babylonian captivity at an end, Africans need to unite around a Pan-African New Jerusalem.

What is ambiguous in the song's lyrics is whether Marley is calling for Africa to unite or Africans to unite. The difference is not semantic. When he declares that Africa is where he finds his roots, he is quite clearly situating himself under the term "Africans." He seems to be including all of the diaspora under the term, for he situates all in presumably his primary Jamaican audience under the term as well. What Marley seems to be doing is redefining "Africa" as not the continent, but the people. In doing so, he is placing himself in the vanguard of postcolonial thinkers. That he does so is certainly a positive rhetorical move if one believes in solidarity for this globally crucial ethnicity. However, he does seem to be abandoning Jamaica somewhat. Where has Trench Town gone in Marley's rhetoric?

"ZIMBABWE"

Much of the world's attention when Marley wrote "Zimbabwe" was on South Africa. There, a racist minority government was oppressing people of color; and the story was increasingly drawing both media coverage and international sanctions. So, why did Marley write about a lesser story?

Zimbabwe is, of course, the former Rhodesia, which was once Southern Rhodesia. Colonized by the British (or, perhaps more accurately, the entrepreneurial Cecil Rhodes), the country had attracted a fair number of white settlers. As Great Britain in the 1960s and 1970s pushed African nations toward independence and majority rule, the settlers in Rhodesia resisted. Eventually, they set up a white supremacist state that was just as oppressive as the Afrikaner one in South Africa. Perhaps because this Rhodesia was smaller or perhaps because it was not as wealthy, the anti-racism cause there did not draw the attention it did in South Africa. Also, deflecting from the anti-racism cause was the fact that the Ian Smith government was defying British directives: it was a rebellious state as well as a racist one; the defiance of Britain drew headlines away from the white supremacy.

In the late 1970s, civil war in Rhodesia was prevented through negotiations. Although the political situation was very tense, it looked as if a black majority government would take over in the nation. Marley's song celebrates this: Africans have liberated Zimbabwe, he sings. The song, however, is not just a song in celebration of an African Zimbabwe. Two different revolutionary groups had opposed Ian Smith's government there, ZAPU and ZANU; and, as is often the case, after they defeated (eventually through negotiations) the common enemy, they began fighting over who should rule the country.

The Marley song is occasioned by this in-fighting. The singer calls for an end to the African-against-African power struggle. That struggle could only succeed in dividing the country and tearing what should be a glorious new African place into pieces. Marley believed in African unity: that meant putting personal or tribal gain aside in favor of the African cause. He was in the song calling on Joshua Nkomo and Robert Mugabe to unite. At the end of song, Marley suggests that we will find out if these two rivals are true real revolutionaries only when we see if they do indeed put Africa first.

CONCLUSION

The eleven songs considered in this chapter span but fifteen years. The political progression would suggest far longer, for Marley moves from being a singer concerned about his people in Trench Town of Kingston to a crusader for an African unity that connects all of Africa's people, no matter where they now reside, and that should encourage revolution against the vestiges of colonialism and racism not squabbles between or among "wannabe big men." Part of the explanation for this progression is that Marley grew older and wiser, but that is only part.

The progression is more accurately explained by two major shifts in his thinking. The first was a shift from believing in communication as advocacy to believing in action as communication. Marley initially thought his songs could lead the people forward. He eventually came to see that his singing—as politically charged speech acts matched by the acts of others—could be a force for change against the resistances that had emerged. His speech acts would remain nonviolent; however, he became well aware that the acts that others might match to his rhetoric could indeed become violent if necessary. Marley, then, was not an advocate of violence, but he was one who saw that violence might be necessary. My reading of his songs suggests to me that he never totally lost faith in the power of rhetoric. However, at the same time, he realized that rioting and looting might prove to be useful speech acts communicating a people's anger and frustration. "One Love" was always the aim, but Marley knew that the road to that aim could be rocky.

The second was a shift from seeing Jamaica's problems as Jamaica's problems to seeing them as part of global racism and global oppression directed against African people. Thus, he began singing more about racism than about Trench Town and, later, more about Africa than about his Afro-Caribbean island. Marley was not alone in making this shift, but he was a powerful, popular voice, whereas others who had preceded him in embracing Africa were either too purely political or too academic. For example, Bajan poet Edward Kamau Braithwaite's *The Arrivants* (1973) makes much the same point about Africans by uniting voices of Africa, voices from the islands, and voices from the United States as if they were one people. Comparatively few read Brathwaite, whereas Marley, even though he died young, commanded a worldwide following. Braithwaite's epic poem is incredibly important in Afro-Caribbean literature: it makes an important political statement by uniting African people in one story as well as in providing an Afro-Caribbean poetic counterpoint to the lyrics of the more famous Derek Walcott, whose style was pronouncedly that of the metropolitan center.

The Bob Marley memorial statue in Kingston is probably read by most as signifying that he brought fame to the land. More people know Jamaica, thanks to Marley's music. Some, recognizing that memorializing statues usually are for political fame not record sales, might point to the "One Love" concert and Marley's noble attempt to bring the warring PNP and JLP factions together for the sake of the nation's people. Marley himself, if he could be asked about the statue, would probably dismiss both the record sales and the "One Love" concert. He would want the statue to recall three things: first, that he had told the poor people of Jamaica that they deserved economic justice; second, that he had told them that it would not necessarily be easy to gain it; and, third, that he had told them that they were part of a much larger African picture in both suffering oppression and fighting for their rights.

NOTES

1. A good account of the different musical styles that have emerged from the Caribbean is Peter Manuel's *Caribbean Currents: Caribbean Music from Rumba to Reggae* (Philadelphia: Temple University Press, 1995).

2. The best biography of Marley is probably Tim White's *Catch a Fire: The Life of Bob Marley* published in a revised edition in 2006 by Holt.

3. A good study much more attentive to the poetic nuances is Kwame Dawes's *Bob Marley: Lyrical Genius* (2007).

FIVE

Images of Africa

This chapter asks, initially, that you return in memory or in history to 1961. In his inaugural as president of the United States, John F. Kennedy suggested that the torch had been passed, that a new generation of leaders were assuming power, and that both domestically and internationally affairs would soon be quite different from what they had been before 1961. Kennedy's general observation was very true in the case of Africa.

There, an increasing number of nations were leaving colonialism behind and becoming independent entities. For the most part, they accepted the names and boundaries they had been given in the late nineteenth century by European powers. These new African nations' doing so helped people elsewhere who were trying to keep up with the changing African political situation. Most people, however, were still holding onto stereotypes about Africa, not even paying much attention to the artificial borders.

One stereotype was somewhat true: there was a difference between Africa South of the Sahara and Africa North of the desert. North, the people were predominantly Islamic, and their skin color was not exceptionally dark. The landscape was barren; pyramids and camels dotted it. South, the people were Christian or animist (or a blend), and their skin color was dark. The landscape was jungle or savannah; huts and wild game dotted it. As is true of most stereotypes, there was considerable truth in these. Less accurate was the assumption that governments to the north were like those found in the Middle East while those to the south were tribal with a colonial regime superimposed.

The Bible and many ancient history units in high school social studies curricula had given those who were trying to envision Africa some sense of what Egypt and its neighbors to its west looked like. (The movie *Casablanca* might have added a bit more to the picture, along with French

53

foreign legion movies the names of which have long been forgotten.) The picture of sub-Saharan Africa was far less clear, with Tarzan movies probably giving many the impression that jungle dominated when, in fact, grasslands did. The overall picture of the huge African continent was deeply flawed, but that of sub-Saharan Africa was comically so. Americans could not locate the countries on a map, let alone talk about how they differed among themselves.

These nations were acquiring independence. They were setting up embassies in Washington, D.C., and they were accepting memberships in the United Nations. How did those on this side of the Atlantic move beyond the very fuzzy image we had of sub-Saharan Africa in 1961? We moved beyond thanks to political communication, but that communication was not issued by either the African governments or that of the United States. Rather, it was issued by popular media. The news media provided some information. If there were a crisis, as there was in what was called the Belgian Congo in the 1950s, the news media tried to cover it. Often, both text and pictures were courtesy of European news services, for the American news presence in sub-Saharan Africa was quite limited. More information was provided by fiction and film. This information, however, was not so much inaccurate as distorted: it showed only parts of the picture. American audiences, then, received a very partial picture of African politics in the decades after 1961.

That partial picture highlighted dictatorship, political corruption, and racism. The media, particularly film, was offering other images, but, on the narrow matter of politics, these three themes dominated. They offered a political view of sub-Saharan Africa that reflected some but far from all that there was to see and thus established stereotypes and, in general, created an unflattering picture of a region where politics, although often flawed in the postcolonial period, offered good stories as well as bad ones.

UGANDA AND "BIG DADDY"

In the 1950s, Uganda was an African success story. Thus, many elementary school geography textbooks in the United States chose to focus on Uganda, making it something of a fourth or fifth grade "poster child." It also provided a positive counterpoint to neighboring Congo, which was in the news for its political turmoil and dangers. The story of Uganda, however, took a negative turn when Idi Amin seized control of the nation. Many fled; its renowned university weakened; the economy soured. Americans had a vague idea that Uganda was no longer the success it had been presented as in those textbooks. But what really grabbed American attention was only tangentially related to the central African country.

In the summer of 1976, a group of terrorists sympathetic to the Palestinian cause hijacked an Air France jet with a large number of Jewish passengers. After several stops, it ended up in Uganda, at the airport outside Entebbe. As the world watched and waited, the Israelis launched a rescue operation—on our bicentennial Fourth of July. It was successful, and it was dramatic. Such drama almost demanded a motion picture version, and, as it turned out, there were several. The earlier two, both aired on television later in 1976, focused mainly on the victims and the rescuers; however, making an appearance in both was "Big Daddy" Idi Amin, enacted by Yaphet Kotto and Julius Harris.

Amin's appearance suggested that, although he supported the hijackers, he was not in control of the situation. He was brought in by the hijackers to signal that they had whatever legitimacy an Amin appearance might grant. In the films, Amin is puppet in and puppet out, presenting viewers with a sadly comical image of African government.

Amin's garish military costume added to the sad comedy. First, it evoked military regimes of Europe and of old. It seemed out of place on those scores. Second, it looked unbearably hot in a climate that most certainly called for something less substantial than what the Amin character wore. The films were not about Amin or, by extension, African government; nonetheless, they sent a message to viewers out of Africa about both. These viewers further assumed that Amin was typical of the continent as a whole. No matter where one looked, one would find leaders who, based on their girth, seemed to be overindulging in the perks of governing. They would also be somewhat menacing—threatening those who crossed them; and they would be comically militaristic.

The later film to deal with the Entebee rescue was the much later *The Last King of Scotland* (2006). This film reverses the elements in the 1970s films: Amin, enacted by Forest Whitaker, was center stage; the victims of the hijacking and the rescuers were marginalized. The portrait of Amin, however, does not contradict the one seen in the earlier films. He is still pompous; he is still overindulging; he is more menacing because he is less a puppet and more a real political force in *The Last King of Scotland*. The 2006 audience was perhaps more sophisticated than that in the 1970s: the audience might have realized that Amin was not representative of all sub-Saharan African rulers. Still, there was a tendency on the part of some to turn Amin into the representative example. The 2006 film, although it focuses on Amin not the rescue, does not present a portrait of African government significantly at odds with what audiences saw in the 1970s. The Amin of 2006 is certainly more complex than the Amin of 1976; however, he is still the pompous and potentially dangerous ruler viewers saw in the rescue-focused films, and he still may, for some, represent postcolonial African rulers at-large.

POLITICAL NOVELS

The Man of the People

There was also, from the 1970s onward, a steady stream of novels that chose politics as their primary subject matter. Thanks to British publisher Heinemann's African Writers Series, they made their way to readers beyond Africa. Good examples are Chinua Achebe's *The Man of the People* (1966), Ayi Kwei Armah's *The Beautyful Ones Are Not Yet Born* (1968), and V. S. Naipaul's *A Bend in the River* (1979). Achebe's novel presumably deals with Nigeria; Armah's with Ghana. Naipaul, a Caribbean writer educated and living in the United Kingdom, seems to have Congo or Zaire in mind. So, the three novels come from different times and different countries. Readers, however, could easily have lumped them together, for they present a similar political portrait. It is not one featuring overdressed, pompous leaders such as "Big Daddy" Amin; rather, it is one featuring rampant political corruption.

The corruption reveals different facets in the three novels. In Achebe's novel, the crucial clash is between an idealistic, reform-minded young man and his former teacher, who has entered politics and is now known as "Chief Nanga." Nanga is Minister of Culture in an unnamed African country, but, rather than benefit the postcolonial country, Nanga has chosen to enrich himself by holding public office. The young man, Odili, is disillusioned when he sees what has become of a man he once very much admired.

The political becomes personal in Achebe's novel when Nanga seduces Odili's girlfriend after impressing her with his power and possessions. The novel thus shows how inviting political corruption can be. The one hope in the novel, Odili's idealism, is even tainted when he seeks sexual revenge against Nanga by pursuing the Chief's fiancée. He also leads an opposition group, but the way in which his opposition has been personalized taints it. He is not the pure idealist he was at the beginning of the novel. Achebe's suggestion is that corruption, one way or another, defeats the political spirit that ought to inform the newly independent nation. Leaders become corrupt; even selfless idealists become more intent on personal revenge than political principle.

The novel ends with a coup directed against Nanga's government. Achebe was hailed by many in Nigeria as prescient, but coups were to become so common in Nigeria that it is difficult to argue that Achebe knew anything about the two coups coming later in 1966 with a third in 1967. The fact that Nigerian reality matched Achebe's fiction, however, emphasizes how accurate Achebe was on both counts—about the political chaos soon to characterize his country—and other African countries— and the corruption that had already settled in.

The Beautyful Ones Are Not Yet Born

Similar corruption—that during the government of Kwame Nkrumah in Ghana—is in the backround in Armah's satirical novel. The central character, called simply "The Man," is a low-level civil servant who tries to live an honest life. Honesty and the civil service do not go together. Unwilling to play the games necessary to advance, he is trapped in an impoverished existence. His wife resents his honesty; even he feels increasingly guilty about being principled. The climax of the story comes when he and his wife invite a higher-level official and his wife to dinner at their poor home. The dinner is comic, but it also reveals how pompous, presumptuous, and corrupt the higher-level official has become.

The higher-level official is Armah's satirical rendition of the many corrupt officials serving in Nkrumah's long administration (Ghana's first after independence). That government will be overthrown just as the novel ends, so Armah's book seems to parallel Achebe's in depicting the end of a corrupt government. However, Ghana does not fall into a seemingly endless cycle of violent government change the way Nigeria does. So, in a sense, Armah's novel is more optimistic about Africa than Achebe. That optimism is perhaps qualified by "The Man." He maintains his principles, but he seems beaten by the corruption all around him. Even if he knew that arguably better government was coming to Ghana, he would probably maintain his depression and angst.

A Bend in the River

Also beaten down is Salim, the ethnically Indian lead character in Naipaul's *A Bend in the River*. He narrates the story of a postcolonial African country that, like so many, is binging on luxuries after independence. He sees the military increase in power, and he sees the leader, referred to just as the "Big Man," assume more and more power. People find many ways to hide from the reality of the hell the nation is becoming. As an outsider, Salim's role is more passive than most: he waits, hoping that events will turn around. Even Salim, though, in the end, suffers when he loses his shop as the property of foreigners such as himself is confiscated and turned over to Africans. Salim ends up working for a new owner, who is incapable of running the business.

A sidelight of interest to communication scholars is the story of Raymond, a white, French-educated speech writer for the "Big Man." He pens the leader's lengthy, florid public addresses, packing into them—he claims—the sad, justified anger rooted in the "Big Man's" difficult youth. Raymond parodies European-educated intellectuals who think they can add a gravitas to the politics of the "third world." What Raymond succeeds in adding is not gravitas but a wordiness that produces boredom.

Like others who serve the "Big Man," he is discarded once his work proves to be no longer useful.

The one truly noble man in the novel, a young man named Ferdinand, tells Salim and the reader as the novel ends that, "We're all going to hell" (144). That's his verdict for the nation. He wants to return to his childhood; he wants to run away into the bush. Both courses are impossible. He ends the novel bitter about the ruined nation he sees, and the outsider Salim shares this bitterness.

These three novels, written over a thirteen-year period, are set in different nations. Their stories are significantly different. Yet, a reader is likely to blend the three together insofar as they present the same politically dismal image of sub-Saharan Africa. This image would come to dominate how those outside Africa—for example, in the United States— saw African politics. Big men, corruption, and—often—political violence were what African politics was all about.

ANTI-APARTHEID NOVELS AND FILMS

The next set of media products that offered an image of Africa to viewers abroad took them to the continent's southern tip—to a South African nation with a very different political history than the central African nations considered thus far. Whether readers or viewers understood the different history in all of its details is doubtful, but they did realize that South Africa had something the rest of Africa seemed to lack: a politically dominant white population. This fact led to a different picture, one of racist oppression.

There were many black-authored literary works that challenged the structures and policies of apartheid that the government set up in the years after the National Party gained political dominance in 1948. Most of these were published by radical presses in black townships such as Soweto. These presses quickly came into existence and just as quickly disappeared. As they disappeared, the works became increasingly difficult to find.[1] They certainly were not able to gain much by way of international distribution. Thus, these works did not offer much by way of a political portrait to audiences outside South Africa. And, because many of these books were banned by the South African government, their effect in South Africa was also somewhat limited.

White writers were able to overcome bans because they were connected to international publishing houses. Thus, writers such as Nadine Gordimer, J. M. Coetzee, and Andre Brink were able to share a political picture of South Africa with a wide audience. That audience, in fact, may well have been a more international than a South African one because some of the trio's works were banned.

The three writers worked in very different styles. Gordimer's prose challenges readers, and she is more interested as a writer in exploring the psyche of characters caught-up in apartheid South Africa than in offering compelling action. As a consequence, Gordimer's works, although they earned her a Nobel Prize, did not earn her a popular audience. Those who did read Gordimer focused more on the turmoil suffered by privileged South Africans as they faced their nation's political structure than on the politics per se. Coetzee's prose is more accessible, but he tends to use allegory, not realism. Very much influenced by Swedish director Ingmar Bergman whose work Coetzee became obsessed with while pursuing graduate work in mathematics in the United Kingdom, Coetzee's early novels offered dreamscapes. *Waiting for the Barbarians*, for example, presents political oppression—a repressive, largely distanced government, brutalized victims, and a gradually enlightened local official who becomes a crusader on behalf of the victims. The novel is about oppression in general—in all places, at all times, but it is also very much about South Africa. The veil of dreamscape and allegory, however, prevents readers from getting much of a realistic picture of politics in South Africa. Coetzee, then, like his fellow Nobel laureate Gordimer, crusades in his fiction against the politics of apartheid in South Africa but does so in a manner that fails to give the reading public much of a sense of what they politics were like. And, as was the case with Gordimer, readership is limited because of the chosen style of presentation primarily to those who choose to read "literature" as opposed to "popular fiction."

Gordimer and Coetzee should, of course, be commended for speaking out against apartheid, but Andre Brink was perhaps more successful, for his novels were stylistically more accessible. Brink wrote realistic fiction that, although focused on white characters who discover the horrors of the apartheid government, does present the political particulars reasonably well. Although Brink's work had limited effect in South Africa because both Afrikaans and English versions of his anti-apartheid novels were banned, his novels, especially *A Dry, White Season*, were read by many—beginning in university curricula and extending beyond those—outside South Africa.

Those who did not read Brink's depiction of township life, police raids, interrogation and torture, the murder of political dissidents, palpably unjust legal proceedings, and violent suppression of lawful demonstrations had the opportunity to see it in the motion picture adaptation of *A Dry, White Season*. Although the movie is flawed by odd casting decisions, curious departures from the book, and rather flat performances from the otherwise excellent Donald Sutherland and Susan Sarandon, the film nonetheless offers a compelling, disturbing picture of South Africa's political realities. The book and film center on Afrikaner schoolteacher Ben DuToit and his gradual discovery of those realities. That discovery causes him to become an anti-apartheid activist at considerable personal cost.

The story struck many as similar to the real-life one told in two books by South African journalist Donald Woods. A fair-minded liberal opposed to white racism and black racism, Woods is transformed by his friendship with black activist Steven Biko and by what he discovers about Biko's death in police custody into an activist who is forced to either be silent or flee South Africa. The story of Woods—and also Biko—is presented in Richard Attenborough's *Cry Freedom* (1989). It is clearly a much better motion picture than *A Dry, White Season*. Attenborough's film is perhaps a bit flawed by being imbalanced toward Woods's story, thereby deemphasizing the true victim of apartheid, Biko. This imbalance is probably the result of following, too closely, the two books Woods published in exile when he needed to make money, the second of which, being a dramatic escape story, did overwhelm the idea-heavy presentation of Biko's life and views in the first. This flaw aside, the film riveted audiences not only because of its stories but because of a strong screenplay that was well acted by Denzel Washington, Kevin Costner, and others.

Striking though are the visual parallels between these two anti-apartheid films. Both contained scenes depicting the torture of those thought dangerous by the Afrikaner government. In the one film, we see a custodian/gardener who is simply seeking information about the fate of a son who disappeared during the June 1976 Soweto riots mercilessly tortured; in the other, we see Biko berated for his activism and brutalized to death by the nation's security forces. Both films contained trial scenes—an inquest into Gordon Ngubene's death in custody in *A Dry, White Season* and an inquest into Steve Biko's death in *Cry Freedom*—in which the nation's pretense at justice is revealed in a darkly comical manner. Both films contained lengthy, accurate renditions of the June 16 Soweto "uprising" among schoolchildren, demonstrations that South African security forces suppressed with deadly force.

These parallels are to some extent the consequence of both films being based on South African realities. Torture and injustice did occur, and, on June 16, 1976, hundreds of unarmed South African schoolchildren protesting being forced to learn in Afrikaans, the oppressors' language, were killed. The parallels, though, had the effect of making some viewers think they were watching the same film twice, thereby reinforcing the images and messages. These were, of course, orchestrated to create a strong wave of anti-apartheid sentiment wherever the films were screened. They also, as a corollary, offered a snapshot of what government was like in South Africa. Based on the films, a viewer would assume that the police and the courts—the forces of law and order—were conspiring to deny the black majority in the nation the right to live in anything other than a subservient role. If you were black and asked questions or made speeches, you would soon be dead. Furthermore, a viewer would assume that the forces of law and order would fairly quickly turn its wrath on any white South African who did not follow "the program" and accept whatever actions the government took as necessary.

In 1961, sub-Sahran Africa was largely a blank page in the eyes of those abroad in places like the United States. Fiction and film had the potential to fill in the blank with images that were presumably accurate because the artifacts were not the fanciful creations of artists' imaginations but, rather, reflections of African realities. Government in the sub-Saharan nations was too often led by pompous tyrants, "big men" who were enriching themselves. The governments were corrupt, top to bottom, with bureaucracies that benefited the few who were employed within them and had the "smarts" not to question how power was being enacted in the postcolonial period. In the case of South Africa, the government was not that of dictatorial "big men" and corrupt governmental structures; rather, it was one characterized by intense racism and police power dedicated to preserving benefits tied to one's race.

That there was some truth behind these stereotypical images gave the images a staying power. The images lacked nuance, painting with a broad brush that ignored the differences that existed among African states that might, to a point, fit the picture. Ghana was, for example, quite different from Nigeria as far as politics or government is concerned. Ghana was stable, and, after the period represented in Armah's novel, less corrupt. Nigeria, on the other hand, has remained unstable since independence. Government change there has been continual with frequent problems arising among the three major ethnic groupings, Yoruba, Igbo, and Hausa, that comprise the European-created state. Nigeria saw the secession of one grouping in the 1960s and responded to it with suppression by the dominant other two; more recently, Nigeria has seen increased tension along Islamic-Christian lines. Ghana, without as pronounced ethnic divisions, has avoided such civil strife; however, Ghana has not had the economic benefits of being an OPEC nation. The story of Congo/Zaire/Congo is a still different one, as it name changes might suggest; and Uganda has moved on—along a fairly positive trajectory—since Amin.

So, lumping together the Ghana of Armah, the Nigeria of Achebe, the Zaire of Naipaul as well as the Idi Amin ruled Uganda of several films distorts important political differences. Furthermore, the stereotypical political images do not reflect still different stories that might be told about such places as Liberia in the west, Kenya in the east, and Zambia (once Northern Rhodesia) in the south.

There was, of course, considerable truth in the separate picture of South Africa that emerges, but the South African image points to a second problem of these media-formed images of Africa: not only did they over-simplify, they gave a consistently negative impression. The sub-

Saharan Africa a reader or viewer might create was populated by dictators, corrupt bureaucrats, and racist oppressors. Again, there is some
truth to this picture, but only some. One would not, for example, form
one's view of European politics by considering only a handful of the
nations there. One would grant, going in, that what was true in France
might not be so in Poland and that Sweden is likely to be politically very
different from Italy or Greece. Europe covers a small geographical area in
comparison to Africa, but, for immense Africa, some assume a lack of
geographical political variability. That variability should suggest that,
although there were indeed negative dimension to politics in sub-Saharan Africa, there might also be some positive ones.

What then does the simplicity and the negativity do to the study of
political communication in sub-Saharan Africa? Media scholars usually
talk about such concepts as agenda setting and framing as ways the media affects consumers of political information. So, media tells consumers
what to look for and in what contexts to put what one sees. Let's apply
these concepts not to the consuming public but to political communication scholars. They—I would suggest—may well be directed by media in
how they study political communication in sub-Saharan Africa. Media
images may well be telling them what to look at and how to contextualize
what they see. Zambia is, arguably, an African success story; thus, it
rarely finds its way into the news since the news tends to cover crises.
What if a political communication scholar was looking at governmental
messages in Zambia? We are undoubtedly more sophisticated about Africa now than in previous decades, so let's take the question back in time a
bit. The scholar might have looked for evidence of dictatorial power,
evidence of corruption, and evidence of oppressive policing. If hints of
these elements were found, the scholar might have—largely inadvertently—offered commentary that evoked images derived from elsewhere in
Africa—filtered through popular media—that only partially applied to
Zambia if at all. Imagine, by analogy, reporting on political communication in Italy in a manner skewed by images derived from Sweden but
distorted by the story and entertainment needs of popular media artists.
Novels and films then may well have done agenda setting and framing
that entrapped not just the general public but political communication
scholars who tried to consider what was going on in African governance
or elections.

Political communication is, of course, the subject here, but one might
also ponder how the simple, negative view might have affected U.S. policy toward Africa. After all, in 1961, the United States had to create from
scratch a policy for the most part since, through the 1950s, African states
were treated as colonial possessions and, if we had any dealings with,
let's say, Nigeria, we had them through the British government. Our
policy was very much entrapped within the assumptions of a dying colonial system. When the United States had to start thinking of sub-Saharan

Africa as separate sovereign states, not some European nation's possessions, how did the United States develop the pictures needed to understand these new nations?

Certainly, those at the U. S. Department of State had some expertise on Africa. There may well have been fewer African experts than those for other parts of the world, but, certainly, the agency was not without people who knew the differences large and small that would distinguish a Nigeria from a Kenya, a Ghana from a Zambia. However, did this expertise travel beyond Foggy Bottom? Were other key players in the foreign policy process imprisoned within the images of Africa that the popular media were creating? The answer is of course a matter of conjecture, but a reasonable conjecture is that these media images, because powerful, probably did influence more people than just the less-informed general public. The United States, after all, did not proceed in its dealings with former colonies and possessions throughout the globe without some misunderstandings and miscalculations. Those mistakes in the case of sub-Saharan Africa could well be premised on the communication about the continent which was being offered through the popular media. Thus, that media in this case may have had more power to shape affairs than usually the case. Sub-Saharan Africa was something of a blank slate in 1961. Media communication may well have written on that slate quickly, before better informed, more thoughtful authors had the opportunity to communicate a fuller, more accurate picture of Africa's governments and politics.

NOTE

1. For accounts of this body of work, see Ursula Barnett's *A Vision of Order: A Study of Black South African Literature in English (1914–1980)*; Piniel Viriri Shava's *A People's Voice: Black South African Writing in the Twentieth Century*; and my *The Lion on the Freeway: A Thematic Introduction to Contemporary South African Literature in English.*

SIX

Kibaki's Failed Inaugurating Rhetoric

Scholarly work in political communication, whether rhetorical or empirical, has focused on national politics in the United States. Only occasionally have scholars looked beyond the borders, despite the rather obvious fact that there is political communication in every nation. One barrier is language; however, there are many English-speaking nations one might examine. Another barrier—one that has not been thoroughly explored— is that most of the lenses through which we see political communication are derived from studies, regardless of methodology, focused on the United States and tied to texts delivered in the United States. To what extent—one must ask—are lenses based on these studies and these texts applicable to other nations.

One body of political communication scholarship deals with genre. Karlyn Kohrs Campbell and Kathleen Hall Jamieson in *Deeds Done in Words* (1990) defined several presidential genres. Then, they updated that work in *Presidents Creating the Presidency: Deeds Done in Words* (2008). Others have explored other genres that rhetors other than presidents occasionally use such as the apology and the commemoration. Certainly, some of these political genres have analogues abroad. Considering these analogues critically advances our understanding of political communication in two inversely related ways. First, examining texts from abroad using the lens of existing American genres may alert scholars to dimensions of those texts that they otherwise might not adequately note. One needs, of course, to be cautious in applying American-based definitions to foreign artifacts. One needs to keep in mind differences in both politics and culture among nations. However, if this caution is kept in mind, one can discern much about how political communication succeeds and fails in foreign lands. Second, one might also see the extent to which the extant definitions are U.S.-specific, leading to a broader and better definition of the genre. So, an analysis both allows one to better understand the rhetorical nuances of an artifact from abroad and gives one a broader understanding of the genre because its manifestations outside the political context of the United States can be discerned.

This chapter then begins with Campbell and Jamieson's definition of the inaugural. At the onset, it suggests that one should think in terms of "inaugurating" rhetoric not the inaugural per se, for not all nations feature a speech exactly like our quadrennial one. Yet, they do have speeches that begin a government's work, and these speeches have an exigence much like that of the inaugural.

KENYA

The African nation of Kenya has had three presidents in its postcolonial history. The first, Jomo Kenyatta, was a popular revolutionary figure, and he sustained that popularity throughout his term in office. His successor, Daniel arap Moi, was elected because he was Kenyatta's deputy. However, he was from a different tribal group, and, in Kenya, tribal differences matter. As journalist Michaela Wrong suggests in her *It's Our Turn to Eat*, tribal differences determine patronage, and, sometimes, they can erupt in violence.[1] Moi's government was, thus, troubled from the start, for his people expected patronage to shift from Kenyatta's tribe to Moi's, and, when it did, Kenyatta's people became resentful. Then, other forms of corruption grew, creating considerable sentiment in the nation as a whole for a change. Mwai Kibaki's election in 2002 was seen by many as a signal of change. Although there were fears that the election itself would be corrupt, international observers commended its fairness. So, there were high expectations when Kibaki gave an actual inaugural address on December 30, 2002. Yes, he might shift patronage back from the Kalenjin to the Kikuyu, but it was hoped that he and his advisors had learned from Moi's presidency that patronage had to be shared somewhat and that corruption in general was to be avoided.

As the following analysis of that address will suggest, that speech responds to the exigence in ways that are positive and ways that are negative. The negative ways—most noticeably its weak embrace of all the nation's people—are, in retrospect, ominous indications of what will soon go wrong in the Kibaki administration.

As Wrong notes, Kibaki proves to be a weak leader. Somewhat advanced in age, Kibaki, despite his public professions, allowed aides to follow the same corrupt path as Moi. The corruption was evident in patronage as well as in attempts to manage public information so that the corruption was not evident to the people. Not surprisingly, the positive feelings at the 2002 election faded, making the 2007 election tense.

That election was, arguably, won by Kibaki's opponent. However, the results were massaged so that Kibaki was declared victorious. There were protests—violent ones. Eventually, the international community (especially the U.N. Secretary-General) intervened and helped Kenya restructure its government in a manner that gave both Kibaki and his 2007 opponent a role in it. Since then, the nation has stabilized.

Kibaki did not give an inaugural address per se after the 2007 election. One was scheduled, but violence preempted it. However, he did deliver an "acceptance speech" on December 31; and, in most respects, it fits the definition of an inaugural. The exigence in 2007 was, however, different than in 2002, requiring rhetorical work that, perhaps, an address could not perform. The 2007 speech, although fitting the definition, is a weak one. Besides not providing much by way of inspiration, the address treats the nation's political crisis in disingenuous language and repeats the ego-focus noticeable in the 2002 inaugural.

INAUGURATING RHETORIC

Campbell and Jamieson come closer to defining, characteristic by characteristic, the inaugural than most of the genres they discuss. Still, they back off from offering a rhetorical formula. They, instead, suggest several exigencies that give rise to the genre's recurring features. First, the genre enacts the ritual of passing power from leader to leader. This ceremonial function gives the genre the somewhat formal, rather impersonal characteristics of epideictic discourse. Second, the genre unites the people, a step often necessary because a political campaign can divide the people along partisan lines. Sometimes, in uniting the people, the genre redefines the people; and this redefinition can serve the rhetorical business of pushing the people down a political path desired by the incoming leader. Third, the genre presents the general principles that will define the new government. Some inaugurals are philosophical; others, more practical; but the genre does not point to specific policy directions the way, for example, a State of the Union speech in the U.S. context does. Inaugurating rhetoric, whether embodied in an inaugural or some similar kind of speech, typically responds to these three exigencies of ritualistically passing on power, uniting the people (defining that term), and announcing a governing philosophy.

KIBAKI IN 2002

Kibaki's 2002 inaugural address accomplishes the first and the third, but fails at the second. Let's consider these characteristics in this order.

His initial paragraph has a ritualistic quality as he announces that "all of us, both young and old, men and women, Kenyans of every ethnic group, race, or creed, have embarked on a journey to a promising future with unshakeable determination and faith in God and in ourselves."[2] His concluding paragraph sounds similar. In it, he pledges "to lead you to create a country you can be proud of again" and he calls upon his audience "to join hands and remain united for the sake of our country" so that "Kenya will be a happy place for all of us." He says that this "is my dream" and concludes by invoking God's blessing.

The only "off" note in these paragraphs would be the word "again." With it, Kibaki suggests that Kenya had not been a country to be proud of prior to this election. Implicit in that, as well as in an earlier vague reference to "human errors" and "certain deliberate actions or policies of the past that continue to have grave consequences on the present," is an indictment of the Moi government. In the next paragraph, Kibaki refers to "[t]he era of 'anything goes'" and to "[g]overnment . . . run on the whims of individuals." And in the next paragraph, he refers to "years of misrule and ineptitude." So, there is in the address oppositional rhetoric that runs counter to the language at its beginning and end that suggest a shared journey with joined hands. To the extent that oppositional rhetoric is discerned, the speech becomes less unifying.

After talking about the "years of misrule," Kibaki offers a paragraph-long exposition of his philosophy of government. Government, as he sees it, is to serve the people by enacting laws and policies "for the general good of the people." In line with this philosophy, Kibaki announces, in the next paragraph, that "[c]orruption will now cease" and, in the following two paragraphs, that his attention will be focused on improving the nation's economy. He then offers a bulleted list, which offers some specifics: "affordable healthcare," "increased tourism," "[p]rivatization [of] non-performing public enterprises," "[i]mprovement of security." He then pledges to work with both the private sector and Kenya's "external partners," to "use tax revenues transparently," and to "play a leading role in East Africa, Africa, and the world." He offers some specifics about the Kibaki foreign policy, but, as was the case with his domestic specifics, they are not overly-detailed. Implicit in a few remarks Kibaki makes about what his government will do is criticism of his predecessor Moi, but it is veiled.

So, as suggested earlier, Kibaki succeeds fairly well in enacting the ritual and very well in announcing what his government will do. The problem is that he does not unite the people. Kibaki's address in this regard goes off course in three ways. The first has already been mentioned: he attacks his political opponents. No matter how small the opposed party's vote was and no matter how low public opinion of Moi had sunk, the opposition needed to be embraced if at all possible. Not only does Kibaki not do this, but he—second mistake—explicitly unites just the members of his party. He begins his fourth paragraph by stating that, "The National Rainbow Coalition represents the future of Kenya politics. NARC is the hope of this country. Our phenomenal success in so short a time is proof that working together in unity, we can move Kenya forward." He then—next paragraph—talks about how many have predicted "vicious in-fighting" on the part of NARC after its victory, but he says "When a group of people come together over an idea or because of a shared vision, such a group can never fail or disintegrate. NARC will never die as long as the original vision endures." If he is correct, then Kenya has a united NARC but not a united nation. Perhaps, Kibaki's focus on uniting an anti-Moi coalition after the election—one exigence—has prevented him from focusing on uniting the nation as a whole—another exigence.

Kibaki's third mistake is the most striking in the address—the speech's egocentricity. Consider the instances of his use of the first person singular pronoun versus the first person plural in table 6.1.

If a speech is to unite the people, the plural should dominate, but it clearly does not. In addition, there are points in the speech where the ego-focus in extremely high: the first three paragraphs; the thirteenth and fourteenth where he begins talking about what his government will do; and the twenty-second where he waxes eloquently about his vision for Kenya. In that paragraph, he places himself "atop Mount Kenya surveying the landscape," like a Moses who will be able to enter the promised land. Or—as he puts it in paragraph seven—like a Moses who "you have asked . . . to lead this nation out of the present wilderness and malaise into the promised land." The hubris is considerable and striking.

KIBAKI IN 2007

That hubris, together with the greed of those who surrounded Kibaki as president, played a role in creating a government that the voters seemed ready to topple in 2007. Kibaki, though, was declared the winner in that disputed election. Before violence engulfed the nation, he spoke on December 30 in a speech that served as an inaugural. The ritualistic elements are less noticeable but still present: he accepts what he deems the people's verdict in the speech's beginning, and calls for peace and harmony and declares a public holiday in its conclusion. Although abbreviated, the ritualistic elements of inaugurating rhetoric are present. The comments on policy directions are also brief, but they frequently are abbreviated in second inaugurals since the leader's administration has long been in place. Whereas those second inaugurals often talk of continuing present policy directions, Kibaki's, however, notes that the voters "have given us the agenda for change you wish to see implemented for the next five years," even though he just before noted that the voters "have given

Table 6.1.   Personal Pronouns in Kibaki's 2002 Inaugural Address

Paragraph	1st Person Singular	Plural
Paragraph 1	6	0
Paragraph 2	5	0
Paragraph 3	6	1
Paragraph 4	0	6
Paragraph 5	1	2
Paragraph 6	6	0
Paragraph 7	1	5
Paragraph 8	2	0
Paragraph 9	0	2
Paragraph 10	1	1
Paragraph 11	0	1
Paragraph 12	2	1
Paragraph 13	4	0
Paragraph 14	3	0
Paragraph 15	1	4
Paragraph 16	1	5
Paragraph 17	1	3
Paragraph 18	1	2
Paragraph 19	1	1
Paragraph 20	1	3
Paragraph 21	2	3
Paragraph 22	6	0
Paragraph 23	0	3
Paragraph 24	2	3
Paragraph 25	0	0
Total	53	46

us a vote of confidence in the values and principles of freedom, equality, and development that we began five years ago."[3] So, there is some ambiguity as to whether the policy direction will be change or continuity. One discerns in Kibaki's rhetoric an attempt to *both* acknowledge the voters' dissatisfaction and suggest that it really did not exist.

So, one might conclude that the 2007 address responded less well to the first and third exigencies of inaugurating rhetoric, noting that the address was not the inaugural Kibaki planned but, rather, the acceptance speech that came to substitute for an inaugural. Oddly, since he is in a far weaker position in 2007 than in 2002, this speech handles the second exigence—uniting the people—much more extensively than the earlier inaugural.

He did try to take the nation beyond its election passions. Early, he says, "I urge all of us to set aside the passions that were excited by the election process, and work together as one people with the single purpose of building a strong, united, prosperous and equitable country." He then says, "I want to commend my opponents" for their strong campaign, and he "call[s] on all the political leaders to set aside their differences." He adds many words afterward on the elections, protesting—one might think—too much that they were free and fair. After these many words, he "call[s] upon all candidates and all Kenyans in general to accept the verdict of the people." He adds, "With the general election now behind us, it is now time for healing and reconciliation." He repeats, "We need to heal," and, then, spends more time discussing how the nation needs to put the election behind it.

Kibaki does deal with the need for unity much more extensively in his 2007 address; however, one needs to ask if more extensively necessarily means more effectively. Whereas in 2002, he united his party and pretty much ignored others, here Kibaki seems to plead for all to unite. A note of desperation is apparent in the length at which he addresses the need for postelection unity. Given this note, one would think he would talk more in terms of "we" than of "I." However, to the contrary, the December 30 address is almost as ego-focused as the 2002 one.

It is reported on websites with longer paragraphs. In its first, he uses the singular pronoun 13 to 4 over the plural. In the second and third, usage reverses to 3 vs. 6 and 4 vs. 10. But in the fourth paragraph, the usage returns to 8 vs. 5 only to reverse to 2 vs. 5 in the fifth and 1 vs. 2 in the brief sixth. Overall, the usage is 31 vs. 32—almost even, whereas one would think a unifying rhetoric would overwhelmingly use "we," "us," and "our." This still-heavy use of "I," "me," and "my" coupled with the pleading quality of the calls he makes to opponents and the public at-large give the call for unity an awkwardness.

A caveat is necessary here. In postcolonial Africa, there have been a series of "big man" leaders in nations ranging from Ghana to Zaire to Uganda to Zimbabwe. With such leaders may necessarily come an egocentric rhetoric. So, the emphasis on "I" over "we" may be a reflection of this political trend. Nonetheless, the egocentricity of the rhetoric does run contrary to the rhetorical goals of inaugurating rhetoric, even if this egocentricity is part of the prevailing culture. The caveat, then, means that inaugurating rhetoric may be more likely to founder in Africa because of the political culture—that is unless the rhetor recognizes that the need to unify the people by suppressing what may be an enculturated tendency to speak of "I" and what "my" government will do.

CONCLUSION

Kibaki's two addresses are inaugurating rhetoric. When they are considered with the genre in mind, both how they conform and depart from it becomes clear. Because the genre is defined in terms of rhetorical exigence, as opposed to a more superficial characteristic such as "high style," departures may well signal a failure on the part of the rhetor—on the part of Kibaki—to succeed at doing the speech's rhetorical work. This may indeed have been the case for both speeches.

Kibaki's limited success as Kenyan president cannot, of course, be ascribed to these speeches. If his inaugurating rhetoric had been splendid, he may well have not succeeded. Nonetheless, one can conclude that his speeches did not help his cause. In 2002, when his election was viewed positively by the majority, he may have weakened his government from the outset by not unifying the people sufficiently behind him. In 2007, when his election was viewed suspiciously by many, he may have mishandled an opportunity to improve his position by attempting to unify the people but doing so awkwardly.

The overall assumption behind Campbell and Jamieson's rhetorical work is that speeches are not just means of communication but acts, deeds. Seen as such, Kibaki's actions at the crucial points in both his first and his second government failed to be what was necessary to ensure an effective presidency. When he assumed office, there were high expectations because of the problems that arose during the Moi presidency. Kibaki's ineffective rhetorical action played a role in his government's not meeting those expectations. Then, five years later, when the exigence was more saving the government than inaugurating a strong one, Kibaki's ineffective rhetorical action played a role in his government's further weakening.

NOTES

1. Wrong's journalistic account offer a good account of the tumultuous period in Kenya beginning with the end of the Moi presidency. See Michela Wrong, *It's Our Turn to Eat: The Story of a Kenyan Whistle-Blower* (New York: Harper, 2009).

2. Kibaki's speech is quoted from www.statehousekenya.go.ke/speeches/kibaki/2002301201.htm.

3. Kibaki's speech is quoted from http://wanjuguna,blogspot.com/2007/12/kibaki-acceptance-speech.html.

SEVEN

The Rhetoric of President Nelson Mandela of South Africa

A Qualified Success

In 1993, the question on everyone's mind was "Will Nelson Mandela be able to pull it off?" The question did not refer to the upcoming election, for it was a foregone conclusion that Mandela would easily be the victor. Rather, the question referred to the difficult task he would have as president—addressing the very legitimate needs of the black South African people, but doing so slowly. The slow speed was necessary to prevent the flight of white South Africans and foreign capital from the nation.

News accounts several years later suggest that Mandela was only somewhat successful. He had improved living conditions for the black majority population; however, he had not done so dramatically. And the nation's economy remained weak. Very few new jobs had been generated. Related to the bleak employment picture was the marked increase in crime (Sampson, 565–68). So, there was grumbling—grumbling that forecasted difficulty ahead for Mandela's successors (Mabry, 36).

Mandela as he assumed the presidency had clearly earned, after a quarter century in prison on Robben Island, the respect that quieted this discontent during the years of his presidency (Davis, np.; Sampson, 495–96, 573–72). Those who followed did not have Mandela's near-martyr status to bank on in counseling a gradual approach to addressing the nation's tremendous inequities, an approach that sustained white capital on the theory that it was necessary for the economic growth that will benefit white and black (as well as colored and Asian) South Africans.

The metaphor I just used—that of banking—suggests one way to analyze the political situation since the 1994 election. Mandela had a certain amount of assets—an *ethos*, which he steadily drew from. As freedom fighter and as prisoner on Robben Island for more than a quarter of a century, he earned that *ethos*. He was—and still is—so venerated by the majority of the people in South Africa that one is tempted to argue that other aspects of his rhetoric really did not matter. My assumption in this chapter, however, is that these more text-based aspects of his rhetoric did matter—if not in his people's estimatation of him, then certainly in how smoothly the democratic nation will steer its difficult course in its formative decades. Mandela's rhetoric needed to establish the ground from which progress would grow. Action to till this soil might necessarily be slow; however, the ground had to be readied. Mandela's rhetoric during his presidency thus had a crucial role to play. Veneration of Mandela, although deserved, will fade to no more than empty words unless Mandela was able through his discourse to begin addressing the day-to-day problems of economic stagnation, joblessness, and third-world infrastructure experienced by most black South Africans. Has Mandela "Pull it off" then might well be rephrased as "Has Mandela established the ground in which a just and prosperous South Africa can grow?"

Assessments of the Mandela presidency seem to offer a very qualified "Yes" as an answer. Davis, Sampson, and the editors of the *Electronic Mail & Guardian* in reports issued in both 1996 and 1997 all noted domestic and foreign policy mistakes; however, these commentators quickly brushed them aside. Anthony Sampson in *Mandela* credits him with producing an atmosphere of stability and normality (495–96). Sampson quotes Bishop Desmond Tutu, former Prime Minister F. W. de Klerk, and former Mozambique "first lady" Graca Machel (now, of course, Mandela's wife), all offering effusive praise (509, 516, 525). The *Electronic Mail & Guardian* rated Mandela 7.9 out of 10 in 1996, citing "his ongoing nation-building and reconciliation work" as a plus and leadership, both "heavy-handed" toward critics and insufficiently firm toward government officials, as a minus. But in 1997, his score rose to a "B," with praise for his "admirable commitment to nation-building, reconciliation and political stability," and in 1998, his score rose to an "A," with praise for his "extraordinary reserves of goodwill" and "his achievement of bringing and holding our fractious land together." According to this source, "Few people in recorded history have been the subject of such high expectations" as Mandela. The *Electronic Mail & Guardian* went on to note that, "still fewer have matched them; Mandela has exceeded them." Gaye Davis's 1997 "No Ordinary Magic" offers a similarly positive assessment:

> His ability to inspire ordinary men and women with the belief that they can and should make a difference has given his presidency a lustre lesser politicians would kill for. . . . When he took up the reins of power in 1994, the world was holding its breath, expecting the racial tensions splitting the country to explode into a bloodbath. Instead, the world witnessed a miracle. Mandela's achievement is colossal.

Mandela's rather limited public policy actions, however, do not fully account for these praising assessments, for the nation was suffering economic and social ills—and a catastrophic AIDS epidemic—when Mandela stepped down from the presidency. The praise is, therefore, almost certainly partially based on Mandela's *ethos*, which he added to by being so accessible and so warmly human throughout his term. I would like to suggest that the praise is also partially based on the rhetoric he used in his speeches. The South African press and populace attended closely to his many addresses. These listeners attended to his words, from his brief inaugural in 1994 to his nearly five-hour fault-finding lecture to the 1995 African National Congress convention to his 1999 farewell. These listeners heeded both the scripted segments he delivered somewhat stiffly and the impromptu asides (Sampson, 495, 504). Which mattered more, *ethos* or rhetorical style, is a question one simply cannot answer, for the two together comprised the public Mandela who, in Gaye Davis's words, "has ensured a stable transition and shown an amazing capacity to take along with him a broad section of society, awakening a common patriotism and unity of purpose." So, although one cannot separate out the effects of *ethos* from the rhetorical effects of his speeches, one can at least give each its due. This chapter attempts to give the addresses per se their due: specifically, to examine closely Mandela's discourse to ascertain what role its very words played in Mandela's success. However, much like his presidency, there are some ways in which the addresses and their words fall short of achieving all that they might have. The primary goal of this study then is to offer a rich understanding of an important dimension of the rhetoric of the Mandela presidency.

Such a study will reveal considerable stylistic strengths that helped Mandela achieve so much. A stylistic analysis focused on verbal content will show that throughout his presidency, he dealt fairly realistically with the problems facing South Africa and offered its citizens boundless optimism. He also made an effective transition from freedom fighter speaking the language of opposition to statesman speaking the language of inclusion and commonality. Such a stylistic analysis will also highlight a glaring weakness: the gradually declining certainty he spoke with as his presidency progressed. Added to this was a second not-so-glaring weakness: a failure to project a sense of activity beyond the normal when such a sense would arguably have been necessary to convince people that their problems were finally going to be addressed.

This study's secondary goal is to demonstrate the efficacy of verbal content analysis in establishing a rhetor's verbal style, especially that facilitated by the program Diction that Roderick Hart has developed specifically for political discourse, particularly for a large body of discourse such as that of a presidential administration (as opposed to a particular speech act). Although this study's primary aim is to better understand an important aspect of Nelson Mandela's rhetoric, the study also aims to highlight how a particular methodology can lead the rhetorical critic to broad insights about a large body of discourse he or she might not as readily achieve if using another approach.

METHODOLOGY

The rhetorical critic has several options available in an attempt to understand what Mandela's many presidential addresses accomplished. Each option highlights a particular aspect of discourse, one which may or may not be pertinent in a given case. Furthermore, some options seem more capable of embracing a large body of discourse than others. And the discourse of a modern presidency is quite large.

The critic might, for example, follow Burke in both *A Rhetoric of Motives* and *Language as Symbolic Action* and examine Mandela's addresses with an eye to how he achieved identification between himself and his audience through the use of aligning symbols. The speeches, however, were spare on symbols. Occasionally, Mandela situated an address so that the scene functions symbolically. Thus, he delivered his Cape Town inaugural with Robben Island (theoretically) visible in the distance; he spoke on labor issues with Kimberley's "big hole" (what's left of a diamond mine worked almost exclusively by African labor) in the background; and he spoke on educational policy at the site in Soweto where schoolchildren protested for educational reform in 1976 and were murdered by police. A Burkean critic would indeed be interested in how the scene dominates these and other Mandela speeches and constitutes a primary motive behind the drama these addresses enact. But the only operative aligning symbol in a large number of the speeches may be Mandela himself figured as martyr, as representative of the African people at-large. Mandela himself seemed at times to invoke this symbolic figure indirectly by referring to his Robben Island prison time or echoing the titles of his two books, *No Easy Walk to Freedom* (1965) and *Long Walk to Freedom* (1994). A Burkean analysis would then identify a few noteworthy dimensions of Mandela's verbal style and rhetoric, but Mandela's language is more often spare, lacking a dramatistic emphasis or aligning symbols.

One also might anchor one's analysis in cognitive linguistics, as Lakoff and Johnson do in *Metaphors We Live By* and as Lakoff does in *Women, Fire, and Dangerous Things* (1980) and *Moral Politics* (1996), and look for how Mandela used familiar metaphorical networks in one or many speeches to sway his audience. Mandela's speeches, however, were also metaphorically spare. Furthermore, Mandela frequently demonstrated that he is not an especially effective user of such figurative language by stumbling into mixed or awkward metaphors. For example, in the Cape Town inaugural Mandela shifted from a metaphor of healing in one sentence to a metaphor of bridge building in the next when describing what his government will do. Later in the same speech, he shifted rapidly from "implant[ing] hope in the breasts" to "enter[ing] into a covenant" to "build[ing] the society" that will be "a rainbow nation." And, in the Pretoria inaugural the next day, Mandela awkwardly used the blooming jaracanda in the Spring as a metaphor for the new nation even though it was autumn at the time and the trees were far from blooming.

A critic might also follow the lead of Fisher and focus on the narratives woven into the addresses and discuss whether they demonstrate sufficient probability and fidelity. But again, Mandela's speeches rarely contained narratives, and the overarching narrative they used—that of South Africa's miraculously peaceful movement from apartheid to democracy—is not enough to explain the speeches' salutary effects, although it certainly played a role in achieving them.

None of these options then offers a way into Mandela's texts that will likely prove especially fruitful, although they will offer some insights. Mandela's use of the scenic, his construction of himself as an aligning symbol, and his use of South Africa's miraculous story are interesting dimensions of Mandela's rhetoric; however, they remain very much on its surface and do not adequately embrace the full body of his presidential discourse. A more fruitful alternative is what can be uncovered through the use of verbal content analysis, as modeled by Roderick Hart in his 1984 *Verbal Style and the Presidency* and his 2000 *Campaign Talk*. Hart's primary justification for studying a presidency or a presidential campaign using verbal content analysis is applicable here as well. Hart argues that words have become crucial tools in the rhetorical presidency, with tonal nuances that suggest the attitudes that the president wants his audience to share. Hart also notes that American presidents have become voluminous users of such words, speaking at a frequency that defies belief. A critical method must be able to embrace that volume while paying close attention to each word but not giving undue attention to a particular moment or a limited set of moments and thereby allowing the part to inaccurately define the whole. Only such a method will allow a critic to discuss a presidency or a lengthy campaign and assess its rhetorical character. If one's goal is to understand a particular address, more limited methods might do; but, to describe accurately the verbal style of a modern presidency or the verbal richness of a modern political campaign, be it American or South African, a critic requires a tool that is simultaneously all-embracing and attentive to individual words such as verbal content analysis.

Furthermore, Hart's success in using verbal content analysis to arrive at interesting and useful conclusions suggests that this approach would be quite fruitful in the case of Mandela as well. Thanks to Hart's analysis in the 1984 book, we know a great deal about, for example, the two different styles used by Jimmy Carter that were almost at rhetorical war during his presidency; thanks to Hart's analysis in the 2000 book, we know that the language of a typical political campaign is not as unremittingly negative as those who decry attack advertising suggest. And, besides knowing that this discourse is not *that* negative, we have a nuanced sense of what messages campaigns do indeed in their entirety convey to the American populace. We know, for example, how public campaign conversation differs stylistically from that of the candidates or that of the press.

Hart's conclusions deal, of course, with the American political system. Although Diction was designed with use throughout the English-speaking world in mind (thus, its ability to detect *labor* and *labour* as the same word), the software does seem so tied to American discourse that one must question its applicability to South Africa (R. Hart, personal communication, November 4, 1999). I raise and respond to this question in the "Implications" section of this chapter, where I qualify the conclusions I have drawn from the verbal content analysis.

For this study of Mandela, I chose to examine fifteen speeches delivered by him during the 1994–1998 period using Hart's Diction 4.0.[1] Given the domestic policy dilemma I saw Mandela in, I chose *not* to consider addresses dealing with foreign policy. Still, I had many speeches to choose from: Mandela, like recent American presidents, spoke often (Hart, *The Sound*). Wanting a range, I chose three per year and tried to include in the group different genres and different audiences, for one preliminary research protocol was to see if there were any differences from genre to genre or audience to audience. There did not seem to be, however. Inaugurals fit the overall pattern I discerned as well as more purely deliberative or epideictic forms. Style varied little from Cape Town to Stellenbosch to East London; from audiences of English-descended whites to those of Afrikaners to those of blacks.

Using Diction 4.0, I calculated the five variables of activity, optimism, certainty, realism, and commonality. These variables are defined and the formula for their calculation is provided in the manual accompanying the software (Hart, *Diction 4.0*), as well as in Hart's *Verbal Style and the Presidency* (1984), *Political Communication Yearbook: 1984*, and *New Directions in Computer Content Analysis* (1998). In the two 1984 works, however, the formulation is slightly different, suggesting that Hart has refined his analytical procedure in the years intervening between 1984 and 1997–1998. Diction 4.0 uses these revised definitions.

Diction 4.0 uses a combination of dictionaries and previously developed and tested measures to provide these five composite scores for a given speech. The activity score is calculated by adding words suggesting aggression, accomplishment, communication, and motion and then subtracting the sum of words suggesting passivity, the number of cognitive terms, and an embellishment score (Boder). The optimism score is calculated by adding words suggesting praise, satisfaction, and inspiration and then subtracting the sum of words suggesting blame, hardship, and denial. The certainty score is calculated by adding words suggesting tenacity, words suggesting leveling, collective terms, and the passage's insistence score ("a measure of code restriction that calculates a text's dependence on a limited number of often repeated words" [Hart, *Diction 4.0*, 36]), and then subtracting the sum of words that suggest ambivalence and self-reference, the passage's variety score (calculated using Johnson's type-token ratio), and the number of numerical terms. The realism score is calculated by adding words suggesting familiarity, spatial awareness, temporal awareness, present concern, human interest, and concreteness and subtracting the sum of words suggesting past concern and the passage's complexity score (Flesch). Finally, the commonality score is calculated by adding words suggestive of centrality, cooperation, and rapport and then subtracting words suggestive of diversity, exclusion, and liberation. Hart has applied this textual analysis procedure to Nixon (Hart, "Absolutism"), Reagan (Hart, "Of Genre"), and the American Presidency more generally ("The Language"; *Verbal Style*). More recently, Hart has applied this procedure to the 1996 presidential campaign (*Campaign Talk*).

After reviewing the data provided by Diction 4.0 on the selected Mandela addresses, I examined the speeches closely with the data in mind. I wanted to interrogate what Diction 4.0 had demonstrated in order to understand what the data truly meant. For example, Diction 4.0 revealed a marked decline in certainty during the Mandela presidency. I needed to look at the sections of speeches the computer-based analysis had shown to be highly uncertain to determine why. Such a determination was necessary because tentativeness can reflect either the caution of the emerging statesman or the despair of a new leader who is finding the nation's problems insurmountable, two very different political profiles.

RESULTS OF VERBAL CONTENT ANALYSIS

Diction 4.0 calculates the variables for 500-word chunks of an address. Thus, for each speech, I have from two to ten sets of scores for each variable. In the figures that follow, I offer the normal range, Mandela's range, Mandela's average, and a note as to whether his use is high, somewhat high, normal, somewhat low, low, or inconsistent. These evaluative terms are defined as follows: high (H) and low (L) mean that Mandela's range and average exceed the normal; somewhat high (SH) and somewhat low (SL) mean that Mandela's range extends beyond the normal but his average falls within the normal range; normal (N) means that both Mandela's range and average fall within the normal range; and inconsistent (I) means that, whereas the average is normal, both abnormally low and high scores occur.

If we examine these fifteen addresses, variable-by-variable, we notice interesting trends.

Activity

This variable measures "movement, change, the implementation of idea" (Hart, *Diction 4.0*, 48). Given Mandela's situation on the assumption of the presidency as the nation's first black leader with a commitment to acting on behalf of its African population, one would expect this variable to be, at least occasionally, outside the normal range on the high side. As Table 7.1 shows, that does not happen.

Optimism

This variable measures the extent to which the rhetor highlights "the positive entailments of some person, group, concept, or event" (Hart, *Diction 4.0*, 46). Given the amazing peaceful transition of power that has just occurred in South Africa and given Mandela's hopes for the new government, one would expect this variable to be outside the normal

Table 7.1. Activity Scores

Speech	Normal Range	Mandela's Range	Mandela's Average	High/Low, etc.
1	47.18–52.46	51.83–60.94	55.12	H
2	47.18–52.46	44.43–51.26	47.85	SL
3	47.18–52.46	51.22–52.37	51.80	N
4	47.18–52.46	48.30–53.00	50.31	SH
5	47.18–52.46	47.21–49.84	48.65	N
6	47.18–52.46	48.24–50.51	49.06	N
7	47.18–52.46	47.40–50.34	48.91	N
8	47.18–52.46	48.87–48.91	48.89	N
9	47.16–52.46	49.23–49.47	49.35	N
10	47.16–52.46	47.81–51.80	49.51	N
11	47.16–52.46	50.33–50.80	50.57	N
12	47.16–52.46	49.29–54.47	51.13	SH
13	47.16–52.46	48.30–52.90	50.25	SH
14	47.16–52.46	50.81–52.30	51.60	N
15	47.16–52.46	49.85–50.74	50.44	N

The score is within normalcy in eleven of the fifteen speeches. Three times, the score is somewhat high; once, it is somewhat low. It does not depart much from normalcy even in these cases.

range on the high side. As Table 7.2 shows, the optimism variable very much is.

Noteworthy is that this variable remained higher than normal throughout the five-year period. There was no discernible dip as the years in office took their inevitable toll.

Certainty

This variable measures the rhetor's "resoluteness" (Hart, *Diction 4.0*, 45). Table 7.3 presents Mandela's scores for the selected fifteen speeches.

Mandela's situation, on assuming the presidency, almost demanded that he be resolute, that he speak with complete confidence. And he initially did. But whereas this variable is outside the normal range on the high side for the early speeches studied, it is outside the normal range on the low side for the later speeches. One sees a marked shift from certainty to uncertainty.

Two different "spins" might be given to this shift. Political activists typically speak in very certain terms about a nation's problems and those problems' solutions. Once these activists become the governors themselves, then the assuredness of their rallying speeches yields to a different tone. As they face what must be done in order to address problems, the assuredness becomes cautious. Perhaps this almost predictable transition

Table 7.2. Optimism

Speech	Normal Range	Mandela's Range	Mandela's Average	High/Low, etc.
1	46.90–52.46	51.83–53.72	52.44	SH
2	46.90–52.46	49.25–55.07	52.16	SH
3	46.90–52.46	53.71–54.82	54.27	H
4	46.90–52.46	45.70–53.90	50.11	I
5	46.90–52.46	53.40–54.40	54.00	H
6	46.90–52.46	52.14–61.00	55.65	H
7	46.90–52.46	52.75–54.20	53.68	H
8	46.90–52.46	51.70–53.15	52.43	SH
9	46.90–52.46	49.61–54.05	51.83	SH
10	46.90–52.46	53.90–58.74	55.65	H
11	46.90–52.46	58.90–61.34	60.12	H
12	46.90–52.46	52.63–61.10	55.89	H
13	46.90–52.46	48.90–53.70	51.08	SH
14	46.90–52.46	52.91–54.30	53.67	H
15	46.90–52.46	53.85–55.18	54.45	H

Table 7.3. Certainty

Speech	Normal Range	Mandela's Range	Mandela's Average	High/Low, etc.
1	47.48–53.50	49.73–54.23	51.70	SH
2	47.48–53.50	51.79–53.67	52.73	SH
3	47.48–53.50	52.80–53.72	53.26	SH
4	47.48–53.50	52.90–57.40	54.55	H
5	47.80–53.50	52.85–53.91	53.30	SH
6	47.80–53.50	54.15–56.40	55.11	H
7	47.80–53.50	49.85–51.80	50.69	N
8	47.80–53.50	50.00–52.15	51.08	N
9	47.80–53.50	48.02–50.43	49.23	N
10	47.80–53.50	46.70–49.45	48.32	SL
11	47.80–53.50	44.80–45.30	45.05	L
12	47.80–53.50	43.27–51.73	47.94	SL
13	47.80–53.50	43.50–51.70	49.59	SL
14	47.80–53.50	42.82–50.42	45.79	L
15	47.80–53.50	44.10–51.10	46.60	L

was occurring in Mandela's rhetoric. This "spin" is a rather positive one: it depicts Mandela making a necessary rhetorical transition. Less positive is the suggestion that Mandela's rhetoric changes because he begins to see how difficult solving the problems will be.

To determine which "spin" is the more accurate, we should go to some of the least certain chunks in the latter speeches and ask if Mandela sounded like the cautious statesman or the overwhelmed leader. That examination will show that there is a bit of truth to both "spins."

Consider the following words from the September 12, 1997, speech commemorating the twentieth anniversary of Steve Biko's death. Toward the speech's end, Mandela drew inspiration from the memory of Biko:

> But our commitment to the unity that Steve Biko stood for will continue to guide us as we join hands in practical action to redress the legacy of oppression. It means working together, government in each sphere and all sectors from society, in bringing prosperity to the province, the country, and the continent which spawned him. It means all of us helping to take South Africa across the threshold of greatness on which it stands. That will be achieved by each of us respecting ourselves first and foremost, and in turn respecting the humanity in each one of us. It means an attitude of mind and a way of life that appreciates the joy in the honest labour of creating a new society.[2]

Mandela's words evoked unity, and they did indeed advocate a moral basis for action in self-respect and humanity. However, the actions called for remained vague. The audience heard what values the action will require, and it heard where action will lead—"prosperity" and "across the threshold of greatness"—but it heard nothing more specific than "practical action." One, of course, does not expect policy specifications on an occasion such as the one Mandela is speaking; nonetheless, the vagueness is striking. There is, however, no evidence of Mandela's being overwhelmed.

In this speech, Mandela implied that there are divisions in South African society. These divisions played a much larger role in Mandela's opening address in the budget debate in the National Assembly in Cape Town on April 21, 1998. Early in the speech, Mandela reviewed the practical accomplishments of his administration. He then asked a series of questions about the expansion of social services. He did not answer the questions. The clear implication was that, although the government had made progress, there was still much work to do. In the last third of the speech, Mandela brought up the divisions within the nation repeatedly. Here are three excerpts:

> It is only too easy to stir up the baser feelings that exist in any society, feelings that are enhanced in a society with a history such as ours. Worse still, it is only too easy to do this in a way that undermines our achievements in building national unity and enhancing the legitimacy of our democratic institutions. We need to ask such questions because it is so much easier to destroy than to build. Other recent developments have brought these observations to the fore, and the ease and suddenness with which the old fault-lines of our society can find debilitating expression.

> I dwell on these matters not only for their own importance. They are also related to what is widely acknowledged to be a certain weakening in the sense of a common national identity that we have been building since we began our negotiated transition. They are related to strains in the consensus we are striving to build as a nation.

> Indeed in any society, let alone one emerging from a history such as ours, tensions and differences will constantly arise. They are the natural internal contradictions in an otherwise successful movement towards a better society. Sometimes they will express themselves openly; at other times they will continue to stir below the surface. It would have been foolish to think that we could avoid such difficulties on the way towards a better society.

Unlike in the speech paying tribute to Steve Biko's memory, here Mandela was speaking in a policy-making forum. His dwelling on the internal barriers to success marked the speech. After these words quoted, Mandela briefly pledged to "continue to advance the basic policy positions of the White Paper on Reconstruction and Development Programme" and to "continue to work for a broad national consensus on all important matters relevant to national reconciliation and social transformation." Note the vagueness of "basic policy positions" and "all important matters"; note also the heavy use of abstractions. Mandela did not sound confident, and, then, he abruptly shifted the topic from domestic to foreign policy and concluded the address by deferring further discussion of specific domestic initiatives to when the various ministers deliver their reports. One might find in this address hints that Mandela was, if not overwhelmed, then at least unable to authoritatively deal with the nation's domestic problems.

Realism

This variable measures the use of "[l]anguage describing tangible, immediate, recognizable matters that affect people's everyday lives" (Hart, *Diction 4.0*, 49). One would expect Mandela, regardless of audience, to stress such tangible matters, since these are indeed the focus of the black citizens who are expecting the Mandela government to address these matters. Table 7.4 presents Mandela's scores.

Sometimes, in early speeches, this variable was higher than normal. However, toward the end of the five-year period, this variable slipped to

Table 7.4. Realism

Speech	Normal Range	Mandela's Range	Mandela's Average	High/Low, etc.
1	48.59–54.37	50.96–57.02	54.63	H
2	48.59–54.37	53.07–53.12	53.10	N
3	48.59–54.37	53.87–55.14	54.51	H
4	48.59–54.36	46.80–50.90	49.00	SL
5	48.59–54.36	51.80–54.90	53.52	SH
6	48.59–54.36	50.82–55.34	52.95	SH
7	48.59–54.36	51.30–53.50	52.53	N
8	48.59–54.36	51.93–55.00	53.47	SH
9	48.59–54.36	49.45–54.32	51.89	N
10	48.59–54.36	49.26–50.15	49.74	N
11	48.59–54.36	49.00–49.80	49.40	N
12	48.59–54.36	47.39–53.32	50.18	N
13	48.59–54.36	42.70–51.30	47.71	L
14	48.59–54.36	46.30–48.92	47.67	L
15	48.59–54.36	43.88–46.32	44.60	L

where it was lower than normal. There are again, perhaps, two very different explanations that one might offer for this slip. The first has Mandela changing from the freedom fighter who hammers away at the oppression his people are experiencing to the statesman who talks more about the general principles that must govern policy-making. The second has Mandela slipping from confronting the very real problems of the South African population—the poor infrastructure, the high rate of joblessness, the dire poverty—to a rhetoric that avoids by offering generalizations or abstractions.

The excerpts already examined would suggest that both explanations may have some validity. There was considerable abstraction in both speeches and there were many generalizations in the latter part of the 1998 Cape Town address. These do suggest some avoidance on Mandela's part of the nation's real problems. However, closer examination of Mandela's rhetoric suggests that realism was still present. There were references—starkly realistic ones—in the first part of 1998 Cape Town speech to the people's problems. Mandela talked about text books, medicine, tap water, electricity, and crime.

A year earlier, in the December 10, 1996, address on the occasion of the signing of the nation's new constitution, Mandela saluted unity, equality, social justice, respect, joy, peace, prosperity, and freedom. He sounded very much the statesman. But, as he trumpeted these governing principles, he nonetheless talked about "homelessness; illiteracy; hunger and disease." Mandela did indeed become more abstract, and he did offer the general principles a statesman might. Nonetheless, the tangible foci of the activist were not altogether absent from his rhetoric. So, in general, there remained sufficient realism to sustain somewhat the activist persona who talks about the nation's ills.

Commonality

This variable measures language that highlights "the agreed-on values of a group" (Hart, *Diction 4.0*, 50). Table 7.5 presents Mandela's scores for this variable.

One might expect this variable to be occasionally higher than normal for Mandela, for he would almost certainly make such appeals in pursuing his administration's social policy agenda. However, the variable was initially quite low—often falling below the normal range. But then, the variable rose dramatically, falling outside the normal range on the high side in the later speeches in the five-year period.

What happened to this variable further confirms the hypothesis just advanced that Mandela becomes more of a statesman. If there is something of the freedom fighter still in Mandela in 1994, it may show up in language that highlights the nation's factions. However, he may, in these early speeches, be recognizing these divisions only to suggest that they

Table 7.5. Commonality

Speech	Normal Range	Mandela's Range	Mandela's Average	High/Low, etc.
1	47.80–53.42	47.44–51.54	49.38	SL
2	47.80–53.42	44.61–46.37	45.49	L
3	47.80–53.42	46.24–48.37	47.31	L
4	47.80–53.42	47.30–56.40	51.16	I
5	47.80–53.42	44.21–51.80	46.95	L
6	47.80–53.42	46.81–50.90	48.64	SL
7	47.80–53.42	44.15–50.82	47.98	SL
8	47.80–53.42	46.70–48.90	47.80	SL
9	47.80–53.42	49.83–49.94	49.89	N
10	47.80–53.42	49.80–53.36	51.32	N
11	47.80–53.42	51.80–54.81	53.31	SH
12	47.80–53.42	49.86–51.26	50.65	N
13	47.80–53.42	49.10–55.90	52.31	SH
14	47.80–53.42	52.19–54.90	53.98	H
15	47.80–53.42	51.88–55.85	54.17	H

be overcome. Nonetheless, he, in reminding the nation of its fractious past, was using language that ran contrary to commonality. He also, in these early speeches, seemed to feel obligated to pay tribute to the many individuals who fought for freedom in South Africa. He frequently named these individuals. This focus on the individual also ran contrary to commonality. Later in his term, he no longer needed to pay such tribute, and he no longer needed to ask people so often to put the divisions of the past behind them. His language could shift to that which assumed that there was now a nation informed by common values. Mandela thereby became less the victor and more the nation's moral leader.

What the verbal content analysis, paired with an examination of the texts themselves, tells us then is that Mandela, as the years of his presidency passed, spoke somewhat less in the starkly realistic terms of an activist and somewhat more in the general policy-making terms of a national leader. All along the way, however, his optimism never faded, and, increasingly, he used language that embraced the people as a whole and saluted their common values. The only negative dimensions of his verbal style are the marked decline in certainty as he began to dwell more on the size of the tasks facing his government and his nation and a no better than normal level of activity.

IMPLICATIONS

Nelson Mandela's presidency is usually critiqued in the media as successful, and, as part of his presidency, his speeches are presumed to be successful. However, a stylistic analysis of these speeches suggests, however, that the success may be a qualified one. There are many positive aspects of Mandela's rhetorical style that help make him, his speeches, and his nation successful. Mandela's early presidential addresses were more realistic than the late. The shift, however, seemed to be in line with a partial shift from activist who spoke starkly of the nation's evils to national leader who spoke more in terms of the general principles that will govern reform. As he shifted, he remained boundlessly optimistic, despite the many strains on the nation and some governing mistakes. He also increased the language of commonality as his presidency continues. Again, he seemed to be shifting from activist who would speak for his group to statesman who would speak for the entire nation.

This shift was vitally necessary for post-apartheid South Africa's success. An activist calls attention to the tangible problems of the group he or she represents. This voice is necessary, for it forces action and counters neglect or marginalization. But this voice is not one an elected president can afford to maintain too insistently without running two risks: the risk of dividing the nation into groups instead of unifying it; and the risk of calling too much attention to tangible problems that are not as easy for the president to solve as the activist had implied. This statesman voice is necessary too, for it evokes common principles that not only unite the people but counsel the patience of a more philosophical, more national perspective.

The variable that very much qualifies this positive voice in the case of Mandela is that of certainty. Certainty declined as Mandela's presidency progressed—markedly so. Although some of the shift may be attributable to his acquiring the caution of the statesman, much of it seems to reflect a growing awareness on his part of how the internal divisions in South Africa will make progress less certain, at least quick, steady progress. That the level of activity implicit in his rhetoric rarely rose above normal adds to the impression of slow progress.

A rhetorical analysis then offers a picture of Mandela as a qualified success. This conclusion perhaps must be qualified just a bit. To the extent the analysis relies on Diction 4.0, it is relying on software developed using a very large database of American political discourse. This political discourse reflects somewhat the diversity of gender, class, ethnicity, and race in the United States (Hart, *Verbal Style*). However, that there most certainly are differences between the culture of the United States (assuming there is such a unitary entity) and South Africa's multiple cultures causes one to at least question whether the software's protocols are completely accurate when applied to discourse from other than the United States.

Three very different kinds of answers can be offered to this question. These answers do not remove all doubt; however, they do make the use of Diction 4.0 in this case plausible and the conclusions it offers highly likely to be accurate. The first argument deals with the linguistic assumptions underlying the program's design. Diction 4.0 uses a lexical not a syntactic database. Therefore, according to Hart, the database is not as culturally sensitive as it otherwise might be for syntax bears cultural markings far more than semantics. In addition, since the program's many lexicons have been constructed over fifteen years by adding words to previously established dictionaries, whatever cultural variance may exist at the lexical level can be reflected by simply expanding the dictionaries' contents (Hart, personal communication, November 4, 1999). The second argument deals with the political context in which Nelson Mandela spoke. The structures and conventions that define that context are very much those of the Anglo-American system. His inaugurals seem quite American; his speeches to the parliament quite British; his ceremonial addresses a combination of British solemnity and American plain speaking. He is, of course, an African; however, the context and conventions are very Anglo-American. Thus, the use of a database that is prepared for the English-speaking world seems appropriate. The third argument deals with common sense external validation. One can ask, based on what one knows through the media, if the political situation in South Africa seems to validate the rhetorical analysis' findings. If one does so ask, the answer is very much "Yes." As noted earlier, although commentators certainly give Mandela high marks, they are also quick to note dissident grumbling, on the parts of blacks and Afrikaners. Many reflect, pessimistically, on the chances of Mandela's successor, Thabo Mbeki, to "pull it off."

What the study of rhetoric adds to the picture is a sense of what Mandela may have done more to prepare the ground for Mbeki. Mandela is a great man: a true twentieth-century hero. Nonetheless, his words may have failed him somewhat. If he had remained certain, if he had projected more activity, and if he had been more adept at using aligning symbols, metaphors, and narratives to strike useful political chords, he might have sped his nation just a bit more assuredly on the route to necessary action. He did succeed rhetorically in unifying the nation and keeping the hopes of its people alive. And this is not a small accomplishment. However, he may have over-relied on his *ethos* and not used the power of language sufficiently to solidify the nation and to give its people confidence.[3]

NOTES

1. The speeches were (1) the Inaugural address delivered in Cape Town on May 9, 1994; (2) the Inaugural address delivered in Pretoria on May 10, 1994; (3) an address on the anniversary of the Soweto Riots in June 16, 1994; (4) an address to parliament in Cape Town in February 17, 1995; (5) an address at a conference on small businesses in Durban on March 28, 1995; (6) an address upon the launching of the Nelson Mandela Children's Fund in Pretoria on May 8, 1995; (7) an address at the adoption of the new constitution in Pretoria on May 8, 1995; (8) an address upon receiving an honorary doctorate from Stellenbosch University on October 25, 1996; (9) an address upon the ratification of the new constitution in Sharpeville on December 10, 1996; (10) an address upon the opening of parliament on February 7, 1997; (11) an address upon launching the National Campaign for Teaching and Learning in Soweto on February 20, 1997; (12) an address on the twentieth anniversary of Steve Biko's death in East London on September 12, 1997; (13) a budget address to the National Assembly in Cape Town on April 21, 1998; (14) an address at a May Day rally in Kimberly on May 1, 1998; and (15) an address at the opening of a jobs summit in Johannesburg on October 3, 1998.

2. The texts of Mandela's speeches are found at the ANC website: http://anc.org.xa/ancdocs/history/mandela.html.

3. A previous version of this chapter was published in *The Howard Journal of Communication* 12.2 (2001): 85–99. This slightly revised version is reprinted here with the permission of Taylor & Francis.

EIGHT

The Rhetorical Success of Thabo Mbeki's 1996 "I am an African" Address

The verdict is still very much out on the Mbeki presidency in South Africa. Whereas the Mandela presidency was a celebratory one for both an African population that had attained full political rights and a racially diverse nation that had avoided conflagration, the Mbeki presidency had to deal with tensions both within the nation and within the ruling African National Congress (ANC) party. Put simply, the Mbeki presidency had to balance the aspirations of the nation's black African majority against the need for the economic resources and expertise of the white minority. In addition, the Mbeki presidency had to effect a transition from the ANC as revolutionary group with a quasi-Communist ideology to the ANC as a dominant political party in a democratic, capitalistic nation (Lodge). These tensions had to be handled by Mbeki with a rhetorical deftness.

Mbeki certainly possesses a background that would lead one to assume he can be as deft as the occasion demands. He handled many public relations tasks for the ANC while it was in exile, and, as Mandela's deputy president, he had primary responsibility for authoring much of what Mandela spoke (Hadland and Rantao). His own rhetoric has, however, received mixed reviews. Historians have noted how some of his public addresses have seemed "flat" (Lodge, 248), and although I tried to defend his rhetoric on HIV/AIDS as strategic in an essay that appeared in the *Howard Journal of Communications*, most in the press and many public officials thought it horribly misguided. In addition, Mbeki's inability to sustain party support suggests that either his rhetoric or his distanced, somewhat autocratic personality—or both—failed him in the end. So, the verdict on Mbeki's rhetoric may well be similar to that on his presiden-

91

cy—still being deliberated upon by academic commentators if not the ANC party faithful.

Mbeki can, however, be considered as a highly effective rhetor. This chapter examines one Mbeki public address that has universally received praise: the May 1996 speech he delivered on behalf of the ANC on the occasion of the Constitutional Assembly's adoption of "The Republic of South Africa Constitution Bill." It is popularly referred to as his "I am an African" speech. An examination of this address is not, however, intended simply to establish Mbeki's rhetorical skill. Rather, it is intended to demonstrate something more profound: how Mbeki as rhetor is able to unite a much divided South African people through a masterful public address. No one has surveyed South African audiences or public address scholars to ascertain what the nation's—or the continent's—most noteworthy speeches might be. If one did, this speech would almost certainly be near the top of the list. It is available online at multiple sites; it has evoked much commentary by South African and African political figures and commentators in the decade since it was delivered; it inspired an operatic adaptation by South Africa's Black Tie Ensemble as well as a rap/jazz one by artist Linda Kekoma; and it is now available on sites such as YouTube and AOL Video in a patriotic 2:02 video produced in January 2007.

In this important address, he uses three strategies capable of creating consubstantiality among the several peoples of South Africa. This chapter will consider those strategies. The more minor two are Mbeki's stylization of American President John F. Kennedy and Mbeki's strategic gradual shifting from first-person singular to first-person plural pronouns. The more major strategy is the use of a narrative with mythic resonance. The mythic resonance lends the narrative an aura that arguably makes its effect more profound. But what is ultimately more important to postapartheid South Africa is how Mbeki crafts the narrative to promote reconciliation by inviting audience members to recognize their common identity as African. Before systematically analyzing Mbeki's address, this chapter will discuss the theory undergirding the analysis, sketch the several arguments about the speech's rhetoric, and reflect on the theoretical pluralism that explains the chapter's choice of melding together insights that begin with different, albeit compatible, premises.

BAKHTIN, BURKE, NARRATIVE

The theoretical perspective undergirding this analysis needs only be briefly reviewed since most of its components are very familiar to rhetorical critics. The perspective mixes the insights of Bakhtin, Burke, and several authors who have discussed the power of narrative in persuasive contexts. Each insight is important, as is the mix.

Bakhtin's concept of polyphony, best explained in the revised edition of *Problems of Dostoevsky's Poetics* (1984), tells us that all utterances entail previous ones. Sometimes neither rhetor nor audience are aware of these entailments; thus, they are without interest—except maybe to a future scholar who discerns them and, as a result, finds complicating voices within a text that alter its meaning for future audiences. Far more relevant are the entailments that rhetor or audience are aware of, for these are connected to the speech's immediate inventional potential. Among these entailments is "stylization," which Bakhtin defines as directed "toward *another's* discourse, toward *someone else's* speech" (185). The concept subsumes allusion, where the reference is to very particular words. Insofar as stylization evokes "the sum total of devices associated with the other's speech" (189), stylization refers the full voice of the other, who is said to be speaking through the text. Using a mix of rhetorical schemes and formal language, a rhetor may be stylizing John F. Kennedy; using a less formal lexicon, strategic pauses, and "well" as a transitional marker, a rhetor may be stylizing Ronald Reagan. "Stylization forces another person's referential (artistically referential) intention to serve its own purposes, that is, its new intentions" (189). Thus, a rhetor arguing at a new time of economic crisis might stylize Franklin Roosevelt to appropriate his call for fearlessness and his finger-pointing at monied interests; thus, a rhetor arguing in this century might stylize Martin Luther King Jr. to suggest a new dream while implying that, perhaps, King's, in its broadest sense, had not been yet achieved. The stylized speaker speaks through the new text, but this speaker is serving the rhetorical purposes of the rhetor.

Burke's concept of identification or consubstantiality is a commonplace in rhetorical studies. Burke sees in this desired state the basis for agreement (Burke, *A Rhetoric*). This may be the desired endpoint to an argument or the communion necessary to unite a group—either by identifying its common ground or by scapegoating a villainous force it can join in opposition to. As I have argued elsewhere, Mbeki may have used just such a scapegoating strategy in his rhetoric on HIV/AIDS. Burke, in a metaphor not often recalled, presents the other strategy, finding common ground, as "courtship," noting that it is "the use of suasive devices for the transcending of social estrangement" (Burke, *A Rhetoric*, 208). "Social estrangement" would be an understatement for the situation in South Africa; nonetheless, the "courtship" strategy is just as available to a South African rhetor as the scapegoating one.

Although the attractiveness of storytelling has long been noted, Fisher's work on narrative (presented in three seminal *Communication Monographs* essays as well as in a 1987 book) crystallized the awareness of rhetoricians about how narrative might be compelling within argumentation. As Fisher notes, "narration comes closer to capturing the experience of the world, simultaneously appealing to the various senses, to reason and emotion, to intellect and experience" (Fisher, *Human*, 75). As Fisher and others have noted, to be truly effective, the narrative must strike an audience as true to reality and relevant to audience members. "Truth," I would suggest, means more than just that the story probably could have happened—that is, that the narrative "rings true." "Truth" has a "higher" meaning. Here, what narrative theorists posit melds with what mythic critics suggest, for stories that evoke myths have, by definition, at least a "higher" cultural truth. Fisher himself acknowledges as much when he notes that "the most engaging stories are mythic" (Fisher, *Human*, 76). (He prefers the moral to the mythic, but does not preclude that mythic might also be moral.)

The most compelling mythic criticism has gravitated toward the classical (Frentz and Rushing; Rushing and Frentz) or toward stories of national importance such as the "conquest" of the frontier in the United States (Frentz and Rushing; Rushing, "The Rhetoric"; Rushing, "Mythic"; Rushing, "Evolution"), the story of Israel's founding in that nation (Katriel and Shenhar), and the historical struggle of the *Québécois* after the end of New France (Charland). Oddly, mythic criticism has not turned to the Bible. It has been the subject of textual analysis (Scult, McGee, and Kuntz), but not studied as either mythic or as the underlying basis of an analogous narrative, a basis that lends a "higher" truth to the narrative.

Mythic criticism, whether in rhetorical or literary contexts, tends to assume that certain narratives are sufficiently a part of a given culture that a few allusions are sufficient to trigger and make the *mythos* a functioning part of text. Nothing further is necessary to establish the enthymeme that one might say the text is offering. The groundbreaking work of Northrop Frye in literary studies, for example, assumes that a dominant monomyth, often in fragmented or displaced form, is both readily apparent and readily functional within texts. More recent work, however, has posited that some rhetorical texts that make use of mythic narratives also constitute that myth as they use it. Charland's study of *Québécois* rhetoric has become the classic case. It demonstrates that the rhetoric associated with Quebec separatism in the late 1970s and early 1980s entailed the creation of an historical narrative for the francophone residents of the province that constituted them as "a people," an identity that the rhetoric assumed they already had. Mbeki's speech, although not as immediately political as the provincial Quebec government's *La nouvelle entente Québec-Canada* (1979), which Charland focuses his attention on, does perform similar constitutive work as it creates a mythic narrative.

MBEKI'S STRATEGIES

Mbeki's address is illuminated by these theoretical insights in the following manner. He stylizes the voice of John F. Kennedy, he creates consubstantiality by shifting his persona to the first-person plural "We," and he offers a mythic narrative for Africa based in the Bible.

First, Mbeki evokes the voice of American President John F. Kennedy. He does so not to associate himself with any particular Kennedy foreign or domestic policy but, rather, to connect himself to the "Camelot" vision, the commitment to social justice, and the highly principled enlargement of American foreign policy vision many associate with the fallen U.S. president.

That a South African politician can stylize an American president more than thirty years dead is indeed surprising. This stylization is a tribute to the image the Kennedy presidency has in Africa. Although we in the United States remember the Kennedy foreign policy in the context of the Cold War, Africans recall it in terms of its recognition of African nationalism and its commitment to assist Africa (and the rest of the Third World) (DiEugenio; Nelson; Noer). Kennedy developed the Peace Corps, doubled foreign aid to the continent, and welcomed numerous African leaders—despite their sometimes radical ideologies—to the White House (Schlesinger). African leaders such as Somali's Abdirashid Ali Shermarke, Ghana's Kwame Nkrumah, Guinea's Sekou Roure, Algeria's Ben Bella, Egypt's Gamal Abdul Nasser, and Senegal's legendary Leopold Sedar Senghor paid tribute to him, making him a virtual folk hero (Muehlenbeck). Six thousand people mourned his passing at a memorial service in Kenya (Attwood); streets, schools, and parks were renamed in his honor after his assassination; and Kennedy's image soon appeared on African currency and stamps (Muehlenbeck). According to Arthur Schlesinger, Africa acquired "a fascination" with Kennedy (559)—before and after the assassination. Thus, his brother-in-law Sargent Shriver noted in 1964 how often Kennedy's picture, torn from a newspaper, was found affixed to the walls of African huts, an observation Harris Wofford found to be still true in the early 1990s (Wofford).

In Ivory Coast, the John F. Kennedy image was strongly associated with the widely covered efforts to eradicate racism in the American South. There and elsewhere, Kennedy was linked with Dr. Martin Luther King Jr. as well as African martyrs such as Patrice Lumumba (Muehlenbeck). In South Africa, it was this link with the American civil rights movement that earned Kennedy a venerated place in the hearts of those opposed to apartheid (Borstelmann). This link was cemented by Bobby Kennedy's controversial (in South Africa) speaking tour of the country in 1966 during which he met with anti-apartheid activists ("With Bobby").

Second, Mbeki creates a point-counterpoint between the first-person singular pronoun "I" and the first-person plural pronoun "We." He begins emphasizing the former but shifts to the latter, creating a blend where he and his audience and others in the nation are grammatically united. Having heard Mbeki embrace historical South Africans regardless of race, they have ultimately embraced themselves as Africans of heroic lineage who are triumphant through the new constitution. They achieve, in Burkean terms, transcendence, moving from a particular racial identity to a broader, grander identity and are thereby redeemed (Burke, *Attitudes*).

Third, Mbeki tells a story that, much like that of the *Bible*, takes his audience through a history of the peoples of South Africa. He evokes Genesis in recounting the created glories of southern Africa; then, he speaks of the peoples who have populated South Africa. Although the story is clearly one involving villainy, he deftly dances around assigning that label to any group. Then, he celebrates the moment of redemption offered by the nation's new constitution. He forecasts a new political order for all of Africa that the now redeemed South Africa will lead. Although the stylization of Kennedy adds resonance and the shift in pronoun usage helps create unity, it is this mythic narrative that drives the speech's course toward consubstantiation and redemption. Mbeki's story is, as we will see, not the only way one might package the events in South African history: Mbeki selects (and ignores); Mbeki judges (and not always as others would judge). He invites his audience to inhabit this story. Its scope perhaps makes it in and of itself mythic, but what really makes it so is the Biblical resonance. He uses that to make it almost inevitable that his audience will accept the invitation.

THEORETICAL PLURALISM

The preceding paragraph, of course, mixes theoretical perspectives if not methodologies. That mix requires a brief comment in defense of a particular kind of pluralism, a comment very much indebted to Wayne C. Booth, who tried to pave the pluralistic path in literary criticism that his mentor R. S. Crane had blazed. Booth rejected both monism and relativism, but he also rejected a kind of pluralism that borrows an idea from here and an idea from there. The pluralism he advocated was one that could genuinely blend theoretical perspectives because, together, they illuminated more of a text than any one did separately. The blending necessitated care, for the perspectives must be compatible. This analysis blends Bakhtin, Burke, and narrative theorists ranging from Fisher to those who view narrative in more exclusively mythic terms as well as constitutive ones. Bakhtin draws one's attention to what other voices are within a text, the narrative theorists to its form, and Burke to its purposes. Together, they offer a fuller view of a text because they approach it from different perspectives. They all assume that rhetorical artistry is largely conscious, but they all grant that much may intrude into a text from language and culture. They all are, in M. H. Abrams's classic terms, primarily affective theorists, emphasizing what a text attempts to do to its audience. One can thus turn to Burke without contradicting Bakhtin, and one can turn from either of them to narrative theorists without critical tension. The pluralistic mix thus affirms all the blended perspectives. It is not mix-and-match; rather, it provides a coherent pluralistic basis upon which to analyze a public address.

A READING OF MBEKI'S ADDRESS

The analysis of the address, which follows, will develop these observations. Rather than foreground the analysis with a discussion of South Africa's political history, I will introduce this background as it proves relevant to the speech's text.

Mbeki begins by telling his audience that he will start "from the beginning." He then intones, "let me begin," and, after a pause, the key phrase in the speech, "I am an African."[1]

In very few words, Mbeki initiates all three strategies. The phrase "let me begin" entails Kennedy's phrase "let us begin" in his 1961 inaugural; furthermore, the phrase "I am an African" entails Kennedy's "I am a Berliner" in his 1962 address before the Berlin wall. Mbeki's use of the first-person singular pronoun in both of these phrases initiates the ego-focus of the address' first half. However, by saying that, "On an occasion such as this, we should, perhaps, start from the beginning," Mbeki involves "we" in the rhetorical event that will ensue. Finally, by saying "from the beginning," Mbeki both signals that he will be offering a narrative and links that narrative to the analogous Biblical one that, of course, starts with "In the beginning."

Mbeki then proceeds with his story. He begins with a lengthy description of the natural world: its "frosts" and "snows"; its contrasting "sunshine" and "heat." He quickly associates the former with a bad time he and others have moved through and the latter with a good time that he and others are now in. The political referents would have been obvious to his South African audience: the bad time was that of apartheid; the good was the move toward multiracial democracy signaled by Nelson Mandela's release from prison. Making them explicit would have unduly politicized what is a celebratory, unifying occasion. Also obvious would be the referents for "The crack and the rumble of the summer thunders, lashed by startling lightening [sic]," especially since he links the storms with the contradictory emotions of "trembling" and "hope" that accompanied the transition from apartheid to true democracy. No need to name the revolutionary force he was an active member of (ANC) or any of the other more militant anti-apartheid groups that steeled the majority of the black population against the Afrikaner National Party government that ruled South Africa from 1948 to 1994. No need to speak specifically of the fears of bloody civil war that had the people trembling and the hope for peace and genuine democracy that somewhat calmed those fears.

This glancing political allegory is quick. Mbeki's paean to nature continues with references to "[t]he fragrances of nature," "the wild blooms . . . of the veld," "[t]he dramatic shapes of the Drakensberg," "the soil-colored waters of the Lekoa," and "the sands of the Kgalagadi." As if following the order of creation in *Genesis*, Mbeki first praises the elements of the earth that preceded animal life.

Then, Mbeki praises the animals—leopard, lion, elephant, springbok, hyena, black mamba, and mosquito. The dangerous and the "pestilential" find a place in Mbeki's praise poem, just as heroes and villains will when he reaches human creation.

Then, Mbeki brings the "human presence" onto "the natural stage." He repeats, "I am an African." He dares anyone to dispute his claim, much as Kennedy did when he uttered "I am a Berliner." Whereas John F. Kennedy dared the U.S.S.R., Mbeki dares those of whatever race who might stand in the path of the pan-African revival he hopes his speech will wrought.

Having taken his audience through a story parallel to the Biblical account of creation, he proceeds to talk about the earliest people of South Africa—the semi-nomadic Khoi and San, who lived in the vicinity of the Cape. In talking about their horrible fate, Mbeki uses parallel structure, describing these people as "they who fell victim to the most merciless genocide our native land has ever seen, they who were the first to lose their lives in the struggle to defend our freedom and [in]dependence and they who, as a people, perished in the result." In speaking of these people, Mbeki offers a story strikingly different from that found in the histories most South Africans would be familiar with. Those histories would note how European diseases killed many of these people, and, then, how the remaining Khoi and San were assimilated into the emerging colored population of the Cape (a racial group of mixed European, Malaysian, and African ancestry that has a political history distinct from that of the black Africans who numerically dominate the country). Mbeki foregrounds what those histories hid: that many of the first Africans encountered by the early Dutch settlers were slaughtered because they could not grasp the European notion of property (and, therefore, stole livestock) or did not "appreciate" the opportunity to work (as virtual slaves) the growing Boer lands. In speaking of these people, note how Mbeki's use of parallel structure evokes the Kennedy style penned by speechwriter and adviser Theodore Sorenson; and note how Mbeki is using the first-person plural pronoun "our" to make the stories of the Khoi and the San the stories of the people he addresses.

The Khoi and the San would be most directly connected to the nation's colored population, and Mbeki's audience is comprised more of the black. Mbeki is aware that many in that colored group did not strongly support the anti-apartheid struggle; he is also aware that, in the 1994 election, the colored vote went for the National Party that had created apartheid, not the ANC. Mbeki wants his black audience to embrace the Khoi and the San and the nation's colored people within the first-person plural. They are part of the South African—or, more broadly, African—people that the address attempts to constitute. The use of first-person plural is even heavier in the next sentence when he talks about how "we keep an audible silence" about these people. The oxymoron in Mbeki's phrase suggests that murmurings of discontent may exist about the fate of these early peoples but not words per se. He dodges the question of the cause of this silence, whether it be the distortion of Afrikaner-authored histories—that has caused many to not be sure about the story—or the political alienation between colored and black—that has caused some blacks not to embrace the story within their more briefer saga of victimization.

The missing words would not only acknowledge the importance of these early African people but would also assign blame for their fate. Mbeki rather noticeably does not supply these missing words of blame—he does not scapegoat—but, in a striking gesture of unity, embraces those he would have blamed. Mbeki says, "I am formed of the migrants who left Europe to find a new home on our native land." Within this group would, of course, be the Boers who oppressed the Khoi and the San as well as later English immigrants to the eastern Cape. Mbeki says about these people, "Whatever their own actions, they remain still, part of me." He embraces them despite what they may have done. Black, colored, Boer/Afrikaner—different groups with tensions among them—are united into the all-embracing transcendent South African group that Mbeki constitutes. Redemption is thus possible when Mbeki rhetorically reconciles these groups with both historical and present-day differences.

Having not blamed the Boers explicitly for the fate of the Khoi and the San, Mbeki proceeds to another group oppressed by the Boers, "the Malay slaves who came from the East." He says that their blood "courses in [his] veins," although it, more literally, courses in the veins of the colored people. He furthermore notes "[t]he stripes they bore on their backs from the lash of the slave master" but does not identify who this slave master was.

Mbeki was walking a rhetorical "tightrope" in this section wanting to neither offend nor absolve Afrikaners. For the sake of unity, he does not want to assail the Boers, the ancestors of the Afrikaners who created apartheid. Rather, he wants to embrace them as Africans within the "new" South Africa. Nonetheless, he does not want South Africans to forget what the Boers did to the Khoi and the San and the Malay slaves many centuries earlier. Furthermore, he wants his black audience to embrace these early victims even though they are the ancestors of a group, the colored, who have not always found common cause with the majority black population.

The "tightrope walking" continues in the speech's next paragraphs. Without talking about whom they were fighting against, Mbeki embraces "the warrior men and women that Hintsa and Sekhukune led, the patriots that Cetshwayo and Mphephu took to battle, the soldiers that Moshoeshoe and Ngungunyane taught never to dishonour the cause of freedom." Mbeki identifies himself as "the grandchild" of these black African leaders from different tribal groups who fought against the gradual encroachment of white (both Boer and English) settlers up the nation's Indian Ocean coast. He also, however, identifies himself as "the grandchild who lays fresh flowers on the Boer graves at St. Helena and the Bahamas, who sees in the mind's eye and suffers the suffering of a simple peasant folk, death, concentration camps, destroyed homesteads, a dream in ruins." Just as he has associated himself with the brave but sad histories that inform the consciousness of the nation's black majority, he associates himself with the painful history that comprises the Boer/Afrikaner memory of how they were treated by British troops during the Boer War. Mbeki is aware of how deeply wounded the Boers were by the atrocities committed by the British and wants to link both their heroism and their victimization to that of the nation's black and colored populations.

Mbeki also brings into the story at this point "those who were transported from India and China . . . to provide physical labour" on the railways and other projects. He wants to tie in one other oppressed group, the Asians numerous especially in the northeastern part of the country near Durban. Without mentioning the name of Gandhi and his South African campaign for equal rights, Mbeki evokes it by noting how these Asians taught him "that freedom was a necessary condition for . . . human existence."

As Mbeki proceeds through his narrative, he only glances at the story's villains. More important, he establishes his connection with all of the people of South Africa, including these villains. He is an African, Mbeki tells us; so are the others. Painful historical and contemporary differences aside, those he talks about and those he talks to are both ripe for redemption.

Then, Mbeki's narrative moves into the nation's apartheid period (post-1948) during which the nation was "torn asunder" as Afrikaner and black African, both of whom Mbeki identifies as "my people," "engaged one another in a titanic battle, the one to redress a wrong . . . and the other to defend the indefensible." Mbeki does not delve into the political particulars such as the National Party victory in the 1948 parliamentary election and gradual passage over the next decade of the various laws of apartheid; rather, Mbeki focuses on apartheid's effects.

Mbeki talks about the effects of apartheid using language that is somewhat general and somewhat abstract. He presents these effects using a sequence of parallel sentences beginning "I have seen," "I have seen," "I know," "I have seen," "I have experience of," "I have seen," and "I have seen." In these sentences, he tells his audience—just to complete a few—that he has "seen our country torn asunder," and "seen the destruction of all sense of self-esteem," and "seen the corruption of minds and souls." Mbeki achieves the linking effect of *anaphora* without the repetition itself drawing undue attention away from the effects of apartheid he enumerates. He also draws attention to the first-person singular pronoun "I," for the address has not yet made its more pronounced shift from "I" to "we."

Mbeki couched his discussion of apartheid's effects in abstract, general language so as to—I would argue—not draw undue attention to the villainy of the Afrikaners he is trying to embrace within his reconciled South Africa. However, when Mbeki shifts from the immediate effects of apartheid to what he will allege are the long-term effects, his language becomes concrete. He talks about "the beggars, the prostitutes, the street children, those who seek solace in substance abuse, those who have to steal to assuage hunger, those who have to lose their sanity because to be sane is to invite pain," and, worst of all, "those who have learnt to kill for a wage." These "kill slowly or quickly in order to make profits from the illegal trade in narcotics" and "[t]hey are available for hire when husband wants to murder wife and wife, husband." These killers, Mbeki says, "prowl . . . among us" along with "rapists who have absolute disdain for the women of our country, animals who would seek to benefit from the vulnerability of the children, the disabled and the old, the rapacious who brook no obstacle in their quest for self-enrichment."

Anyone who has visited South Africa in the post-apartheid period would find Mbeki's description apt. The beautiful city of Cape Town, for example, has acquired the nickname "Rape Town" because of the prevalence of sexual violence there. Note how the poverty and the crime, as well as black-on-black violence in KwaZulu-Natal province between Xhosa and Zulu and the ANC and the Inkatha Freedom Party, are presented as the consequences of apartheid. Apartheid, the abstraction, has had lingering effects on the nation. These effects heavily involve just the nation's black African people. By focusing on them, he is not focusing on the white Afrikaners who set the stage. The former freedom fighter Mbeki is deftly not scapegoating the Afrikaners (or white South Africans more broadly). He dodges the question of blame so as to not blame: consubstantiality is to be gained here through unifying, not dividing, rhetoric.

Mbeki says he knows of these horrors because "I am an African." But he also knows that he—and, he will soon argue, others—are "born of a people who are heroes and heroines," who can triumph over apartheid's legacy. Mbeki tells his audience that "I am born of a people who would not tolerate oppression" and that "I am of a nation that would not allow . . . [the] fear of death, torture, imprisonment, exile or persecution" to "result in the perpetuation of injustice." The terms of Mbeki's narrative suggest the ANC as the heroes in this story, but he does not name his political party. Nor does he name his race. Having previously given himself a heritage that mixes the different peoples of South Africa, Mbeki associates all of them within the group that stands heroically against the horrors. However, to the extent his audience can name names, they provide the freedom fighters' litany, thereby muting any anger audience members may have felt at his depiction of post-apartheid violence in South Africa in terms too black-on-black.

At this point in the speech and in the narrative, Mbeki loses himself (the "I") in this heroic group. Insofar as those before him share the same commitment, they are also part of that group. Once again, divergent groups are united through transcendence. "Whatever the circumstances they have lived through and because of that experience, they are determined to define for themselves who they are and who they should be," Mbeki tells his audience. And as his "I" is joined by this "they," the dominant voice in the speech becomes "we."

And what has this heroic "we" done? This "we" has crafted and adopted a new constitution for South Africa:

> The constitution whose adoption *we* celebrate constitutes an unequivocal statement that *we* refuse to accept that *our* Africanness shall be defined by *our* race, colour, gender or historical origins. It is a firm assertion made by *ourselves* that South Africa belongs to all who live in it, black and white. It gives concrete expression to the sentiment *we* share as Africans, and will defend to the death, that the people shall govern.

Mbeki stops his story at this present moment to talk at some length about the constitution. Again using a parallelism that approaches *anaphora*, he salutes what the document does. He tells us "It gives concrete expression to the sentiment . . . that the peoples shall govern," "It recognizes . . . the dignity of the individual," "It seeks to create the situation in which all *our* people shall be free from fear," "It aims to open the doors," "It provides . . . opportunity," "It creates a law-governed society," "It enables the resolution of conflicts by peaceful means," and "It rejoices in the diversity of *our* people and creates the space for all of *us* voluntarily to define *ourselves* as one people" [italics added for emphasis].

Before Mbeki began to speak of the constitution, there were two groups in South Africa. Thanks to the president's rhetoric, the two groups were *not* white and nonwhite, as one might think; rather, the two groups were those living impoverished or criminal lives as the long-term consequences of apartheid and those who heroically were overcoming these consequences through the constitution. By the time Mbeki finishes speaking of that constitution, the sufferers have vanished from view. The "we" has seemingly expanded to include them as well—that is, if the constitution fulfills its promise. Such is, Mbeki suggests, the power and magic of the document he is celebrating on this day. Such is its redemptive potential. The Biblical parallel is again relevant at this point. Mbeki's "Genesis" story has led to his account of an oppressed people. Now, the story is at the transition point between *Old Testament* and *New*. The redemptive potential of the constitution is subtly paralleled with the redemptive potential of Jesus Christ.

Very importantly, the "we" that can be redeemed is African. Although political scientists might question the accuracy of Mbeki's judgment about the constitution's sources—finding in it many echoes of Western documents, he declares that "this magnificent product [the constitution] is the unique creation of African hands and African minds." He admits that "we" "draw on the accumulated experience and wisdom of all humankind" in crafting the constitution, but, that experience and wisdom aside, the document is African and brings together consubstantially all Africans.

Mbeki admits—in a passage rife with alliteration—that, as humans, Africans are "prone to pettiness, petulance, selfishness, and short-sightedness." These weaknesses could have undermined the effort, but they did not: "we looked at ourselves and said the time had come that we make a super-human effort to be other than human, to respond to the call to create for ourselves a glorious future, to remind ourselves of the Latin saying: *Gloria est consequenda*—Glory must be sought after!" As Mbeki intones his "Gloria," we are reminded of the what in the speech's Biblical subtext occasions the angels' "Gloria" on Christmas night.

Note that, in this passage, the emphasis is still on "we." Note also that "we" are Africans, not South Africans. In fact, throughout the speech, although the story has been for the most part the South African story, Mbeki has spoken as an African and has brought a multiracial, multiethnic group together as Africans.

Thus, after an obligatory paragraph in which he thanks all the parties who worked on the constitution, he turns to Africa. (His move parallels that in the Bible from the Holy Land of the gospels to the early Christian diaspora of the Pauline epistles.) He talks about "[t]he pain of the violent conflict that the peoples of Liberia, Somalia, the Sudan, Burundi and Algeria" suffer from. He talks about "[t]he dismal shame of poverty, suffering and human degradation of" his continent. As an African, he says he shares the pain and the shame. Since he has constituted his audience as Africans, it is a pain and a shame they all share. He said earlier that, "Today it feels good to be an African." Having looked outward at the rest of Africa, Mbeki talks about "[t]he blight on our happiness." That "blight" is, Mbeki suggests, due to both the conditions that exist elsewhere on the continent *and* the fact that Africans have suffered a "drift to the periphery of the ordering of human affairs." The world community has pushed aside Africans from positions of power, relegating them to the margins.

There are then problems to be addressed and an opportunity within the international arena to be seized. With these in mind, Mbeki continues his narrative into the future. It is a future in which "Africa shall be at peace"; it is a future in which "Africa will prosper." And, clearly, South Africa, its people so constituted along the lines Mbeki has traced, will play the major role in an African Renaissance—an appropriate one since the peoples of South Africa are Africans just as Mbeki is an African. Mbeki concludes his speech by declaring "[N]othing can stop us now!" Just as John F. Kennedy used the occasion of his inaugural address in 1961 to signal that the United States would play a much larger role in the world than during the somewhat self-absorbed 1950s, and just as Kennedy used his rather militant "I am a Berliner" address to reinforce that message, Mbeki signals to the rest of Africa the leadership role South Africa expects to assume and to the rest of the world that Africa, under South African leadership, will no longer remain on "the periphery." Insofar as Mbeki uses a formal style heavy with rhetorical schemes that evokes Kennedy's style, the American president speaks through Mbeki. Thus, Mbeki exhibits stylization. The specific phrases in Mbeki's speech that link to the inaugural or the "I am a Berliner" address cement the connection.

One might also suggest that Mbeki was voicing Kennedy not only to link his vision of South Africa's leadership on its continent to Kennedy's vision of the United States' leadership in foreign affairs, but to borrow something of the aura of Kennedy's "Camelot" for the new South African nation, the African renaissance it would lead, and the peace and prosperity that renaissance would produce. The stylization, then, blends with the *New Testament* aura to present a gloriously optimistic picture of South Africa's—and Africa's—future.

CONCLUSION

Mbeki's career, especially during the presidency, has been marked by rhetorical successes and rhetorical failures. Perhaps, failures ultimately dominated, precipitating his defeat as ANC leader and, then, his resignation as president. In general, then, public address scholars might argue about Mbeki's rhetorical acumen. His "I am an African" speech, delivered while still deputy president, is nonetheless a fine one and a very highly regarded one, a speech that could have set a unifying, transcending tone for all of his rhetoric. In his "I am an African speech," he creates a powerful consubstantiality among the different groups that he constitutes as his audience as he celebrates South Africa's new constitution; he announces an important role for his nation in what he envisions as an African Renaissance, a role that seems not only appropriate, but also inevitable for the people who have embraced the African identity the speech has offered them. He uses many techniques in achieving these aims, among them strategically shifting from "I" to "we" and strategically echoing American President John F. Kennedy. The use of narrative, however, is probably Mbeki's most powerfully used technique. He skillfully tells his nation's history in such a way as to bring all of its people together without totally ignoring the villainy in its past. He frames the present as a problem he and his diverse audience together as African heroes and heroines have addressed through the constitution. He looks to a future of African peace and prosperity led by the "new" South Africa.

The narrative Mbeki invites his audience to embrace begins as if *Genesis*. It moves through the stories of tribes and tribal leaders; it talks about prophesies and exiles. After the *Old Testament* evocations, it offers a redemptive story that embraces all. The narrative concludes this *New Testament* with "glory," with a new Edenic vision of African peace and prosperity. Mbeki's narrative, then, is effective not only because of what it includes and how it presents what it includes, but because it echoes holy scripture—what many have termed "the greatest story ever told."

Mbeki's "I am an African" speech was successful. Given its ready availability in several media (something one cannot say of any other African public address), one might even posit that this speech was the most memorable African political address ever. If only Mbeki's rhetorical skills, as evidence in the speech, had carried over to his presidency. That they arguably did not should not, however, detract from both the rhetoric and the vision of the "I am an African" speech. Mbeki envisions a new South Africa and he exhibits the rhetoric of reconciliation to embrace all of his nation's people in that new African land.[2]

NOTES

1. Mbeki's address is available at numerous websites. I am quoting the text available at www.southafrica.info/ess_info/sa_glance/government/mbeki.htm. This text offers no page numbers; thus, page numbers are not provided in my analysis.

2. A version of this essay was published in *Communication Quarterly* 57.3 (2009): 319–33. It is reprinted here with the permission of Taylor & Francis and the Eastern Communication Association.

NINE

The Democratic Alliance

Escaping the Shadows of the South African Past?

Anyone writing about South Africa in the 1980s would have predicted a violent resolution to the conflict in the nation between the defenders of apartheid—primarily the National Party—and its increasingly more militant opponents. Fortunately, National Party (NP) leader F. W. DeKlerk foresaw how events were playing out both in the country and internationally. He used NP losses in an election to redirect the government's policy from confrontation to negotiation; he freed imprisoned African National Conference (ANC) leader Nelson Mandela from Robben Island; and he began the discussions that would result in a miracle that few would have predicted. Mandela put his justifiable anger aside and joined with DeKlerk in a tense alliance that resulted in the nation's first truly democratic elections in April 1994.

That election involved many political parties, but the ANC's numbers overwhelmed all others. Democracy, however, requires an opposition. Such a requirement was in line with the British model; more important, such a requirement seemed necessary if South Africa was to avoid the model too common throughout postcolonial Africa in which one party and, often, one "big man" controlled what was labeled a democracy but arguably was not. Mandela's response to the need was to appoint his two strongest political opponents as deputy presidents. Neither lasted long in the role—for personal reasons and because their parties were not positioned to serve as the "loyal opposition." The Inkatha Freedom Party, brought into the 1994 election very late, was too regional an entity with its membership heavily in KwaZulu-Natal; the NP was too tainted by its association with apartheid.

Mandela was considered by many a saint and therefore difficult to oppose. Fortunately for the nation, his policies reflected an admirable even-handedness. An opposition was not essential during his presidency. But, as the high office passed to Mbeki and then to Zuma, the ANC needed a political counterpoint. The Democratic Alliance (DA) has gradually emerged as that counterpoint.

The rhetorical situation of the DA is worth considering. The ANC insofar as it represented the former victims of apartheid has had morality on its side, making the ANC difficult to oppose. However, there have been some among the ANC ranks who wanted to enact revenge against the white minority through policies of income redistribution and through government spending shifts away from services for the minority population. There was undoubtedly also some of the greed that had undermined other postcolonial African governments. These tendencies required a tactful opposition. That opposition also had to signal its unquestioned support for the changes that had occurred in the early 1990s. So signaling meant that the opposition had to avoid all indications that it might be the repository for retrograde ideas. Those ideas, of course, had not vanished. There were still Afrikaner white supremacists around. Some had abandoned the NP and joined right-wing fringe groups, but these were only the ones who actually voiced the now-outmoded political views that had provided the foundation for apartheid. There were undoubtedly others who thought the NP had a point at least insofar as the NP voiced its concern over the capability of those who would be in charge under majority rule. Deep-seated attitudes simply do not disappear because DeKlerk chose negotiation over violence and voters, 80 percent plus of whom were African, overwhelmingly elected the ANC. Where would those who held such now retrograde attitudes end up in the new political mix? The DA needed to exercise care that those people did not end up as prominent members of the new party; the DA needed to exercise care that their attitudes did not resurface in the DA's positions on policy matters.

Calling the DA a "new party" is, I would suggest, a fact. It developed out of other political parties, but, as its merger and the un-merger with the New National Party might suggest, the DA was clearly not just the continuation of liberal parties that had existed—with minimal impact—under apartheid. The DA was far more centrist than these liberal groups had been. More important, the DA occupied a dramatically different rhetorical and political position in the new South Africa: rather than being a liberal counterpoint with minimal power under the apartheid NP regime, the DA was a conservative counterpoint with minimal power under the ANC government. Many of the principle players had not changed, but their role had shifted from advocating reform to counseling restraint.

The DA's situation was not an enviable one. Responding to the multiple exigencies would require care. Who the DA elected and selected could send signals. What party members might say in public, whether in assemblies or to the press, could send signals. And, in this day, what the party's website does and says could most certainly send signals. This chapter will examine that website, reading it critically, primarily from an ANC point-of-view. This perspective is important, for the DA must be seen as a genuine opposition, asking questions appropriate in a democratic government, in the eyes of ANC partisans. If it is not, then, rather than a "loyal opposition," we have a vestige of renounced political beliefs.

EXAMINING THE WEBSITE

The website has a home page, five substantive sections (about, our people, our policies, campaigns, and newsroom), and two sections that one can click if one wishes to become involved in the DA, one labeled "get involved"; the other "contact." The examination in this chapter will focus on the home page and four of the five substantive sections. The "newsroom" section will not usually be considered because its content is more variable. Of course, all content on a website is variable, but that in the sections considered is more likely to remain unchanged over a fair amount of time. The date of access can be assumed to April 2012, but, if one were to go to these sections six months hence or a year hence, one is likely to find the same text.

The examination will look for eight "clues" that the DA is less the "loyal opposition" and more an updated version of the NP.

First, what languages are present?

South Africa is a multilingual nation. Under apartheid, the two dominant languages were Afrikaans and English. Prior to 1948, the latter dominated; after 1948 and the beginning of the NP's dominance of the government, Afrikaans became increasing more important. There were also many African languages: to a large extent, they were regional. Thus, in 1970, an educated South African, if white, would be expected to speak either Afrikaans or English fluently, know the other, and know a bit of the African language prevalent in his or her area. An educated South African from the other racial groups of apartheid, colored, Asian, and African, would be expected to have acquired the same mix but with greater fluency in an African tongue if African.

African languages were clearly secondary in apartheid South Africa, prompting some African groups—most notably, the Zulu people—to push their language into prominence. But the more politically real tension was between English and Afrikaans. English had become the language of the anti-apartheid liberal press as well as the language of much anti-apartheid writing aimed at an international readership as well as a domestic one. Thus, Africans were typically much more fluent in English than Afrikaans. This tilt compelled the NP government in the mid-1970s to strengthen the position of the Afrikaans language in *all* South African schools. Calling Afrikaans, the "language of the oppressor," many Africans, old and young, actively resisted this increased emphasis. Thus were born the Soweto riots in June 1976: schoolchildren marching against the Afrikaans language became the victims of police violence, and Soweto and other African townships violently exploded in response.

This history explains why a political party must be cautious in using Afrikaans. Tensions among "tribal" groups also festered late in the apartheid era. Thus, a political party must also be cautious in using a given African language. English is the politically safe choice. However, English may not speak to all the people one is hoping to attract to the party. There were, as apartheid ended, some less educated Afrikaners who had facility only in Afrikaans; and there were some less educated Africans who had facility only in one of the many African languages. This reality would suggest that English alone cannot be used, but considerable care must be taken when using—or making available—other languages.

Second, among the roster of leaders, how many have either Afrikaner names or Afrikaner credentials?

Post-apartheid, Afrikaners remain a part of the country. Many have the expertise the ANC government needs, so even the most fervent opponent of apartheid probably would not have wanted all of the Afrikaners to disappear. (Yes, there was the Pan-African Congress with its "One Settler, One Bullet" slogan at the height of the anti-apartheid movement; however, the violent revolutionary creed implicit in the slogan softened quickly once the focus shifted from gaining freedom to sustaining an economy.) Some Afrikaners, in fact, joined the ranks of the ANC. The question for the DA is how many Afrikaner names would be among its leadership: too many and the DA would look like an Afrikaner party. Furthermore, even during apartheid, there were affiliations that might mark one as a "true" member of Afrikanerdom. Marks such as membership in a particular church or political brotherhood would not very likely appear on a party website, but education might as well as government experience and police-military experience. An Afrikaner who attended "Wits" in Johannesburg and served in a benign ministry would be viewed very differently from one who attended Stellenbosch and served in the armed forces.

Related is the third question: is there an appropriate balance among the nation's different ethnic groups: English-speaking white, Afrikaners, coloreds, Asians, and Africans with, perhaps, some balance among African groups or, at least, no undue dominance by either Xhosa or Zulu peoples. The word "appropriate" is, of course, a thorny one.

Mathematics does not answer it, but it does give some guidelines. During apartheid, governmental responsibilities, at the federal and—eventually—at the provincial levels, seemed split between Anglophone whites and Afrikaners. The bilingual government documents and sign-age in the country seemed to reinforce the 50-50 split. But these two groups together only accounted for approximately 15 percent of the pop-ulation. The colored population was 5 percent; the Asian, 5 percent. The remaining 75 percent was African. (I'm using numbers divisible by five here for ease of explanation: the precise numbers are a bit higher and lower for the groups, but a 15-5-5-75 division offers one a reasonably accurate demographic profile.) So, if, post-apartheid, a political party were to reflect the population, in a group of twenty, one should be col-ored, one should be Asian, three should be white (split 2-1 or 1-2 between Anglophone and Afrikaner), and fifteen should be African.

No one expects a political party to match that description exactly. There are reasons why certain ethnic groups might choose the DA over the ANC just as there are reason why certain ethnic groups might choose the ANC over the DA. The DA, however, needs to be *not* overwhelmingly white; in fact, the DA probably should not be majority white.

The next set of questions takes us from demographic issues to policy issues.

Perhaps the biggest fear shared by the population after the 1994 elec-tion was that the ANC would enact radical policies of income and prop-erty redistribution. The Mandela government did, in fact, proceed cau-tiously on this issue, trying to prevent the flight of white capital and expertise from the nation. Still, the ANC recognized the need for the gross inequities of the past to be addressed. One would have in 1994 expected strong opposition to redistribution on the part of the NP, but the DA is not the NP. The DA positions itself as more centrist on ques-tions such as redistribution. Therefore, its message needs to be one of caution, not outright opposition. There is, of course, a gray area in be-tween; thus, the DA is forced to walk a rhetorical tightrope on the issue of income and property redistribution.

Related to this issue is the distribution of social services. Under apart-heid, the white minority received the lion's share of government social service spending. The schools and the hospitals, for example, were vastly superior in white-dominated regions in the country. Again, the ANC was committed to making dramatic changes in government spending, but Mandela wished to proceed somewhat cautiously. The DA's rhetorical positioning would be supportive of this caution but it would have to avoid questioning the need for adjustments in spending for such ques-tioning would be perceived by many as being contrary to the cause of justice.

A third public policy issue concerns who will drive the economic engines of South Africa. The question only implicitly parses along racial lines, but an observer needs to be aware that those racial lines do exist. The ANC believed in a strong government role in the nation's economy. This belief fit the party's socialist leanings. It also reflected its view that economic justice was more likely if the post-apartheid government was calling the shots as opposed to a private sector still dominated by Anglophone and Afrikaner whites. The initial NP position and the eventual DA position stress private sector involvement much more. Implicit in the DA position is a philosophy of government (especially in the economic arena) at odds with that of the ANC; also implicit is a belief that private sector involvement will produce both more efficiency and more international involvement. On this issue, the DA probably has more leeway, for the liberal-conservative philosophical split is not necessarily a matter related to race.

A fourth public policy issue concerns crime. Crime was a problem during the apartheid era. For a period, the government managed to contain crime to an extent within black areas. But it did leak out. Thus, many white suburban homes in metropolitan Johannesburg had their walls, their gates, their security systems, and their guard dogs. By the 1990s, downtown Johannesburg was dangerous for tourists to walk around in. Around the time of the change in government, Cape Town acquired the nickname "Rape Town" because of the increased violence throughout the city against women. After the change, crime spread into areas of the country that had previously been peaceful. Rural areas dominated by Afrikaner farmers saw crime for the first time, and they blamed it on the African population that was no longer confined to townships and homelands. Much of the crime was indeed black against white, but much was also black against black. If one were to analyze the post-1994 crime, one would find that socioeconomic status explained it more accurately than race, but, since most of those in the lower strata were black, many saw the crime problem as a black problem. The ANC had to act against the increased crime, but it also had to shift the focus away from its racial dimensions. The DA, on the other hand, had to call for even more action against the increasing crime but without its call coming across as anti-black.

On crime, there was some consonance between the ANC and DA positions. One would think there would also be consonance on a final public policy issue: the HIV/AIDS epidemic in South Africa. On this issue, there had been an ANC blip. For a short period, ANC leader and President Thabo Mbeki embraced a minority viewpoint in the medical community, and he argued that HIV did not cause AIDS, that poverty was the true cause, and the drug regimen widely supported for those testing HIV positive actually pushed a person toward AIDS. Mbeki suggested that profit-hungry pharmaceutical companies, hand-in-glove with Western governments, were pushing the drugs on predominantly black African nations even though these companies knew the drugs' true effects.[1] Mbeki, widely criticized in and out of South Africa for his stance, later retreated from it. So, as we look at the DA website, we ought to see the party saying much the same thing about the epidemic as the ANC.

Two questions emerge: first, to what extent does the DA fault the ANC for the blip; second, to what extent does the DA raise the issue at all. The latter question is relevant because the HIV/AIDS epidemic has affected the nation's black population, not the Anglophone or Afrikaner white. A de-emphasis on the issue could be viewed as a reflection of the DA's true constituency.

Having outlined the questions, I will now examine the website, question by question and website section by website section.

LANGUAGE

The website is predominantly in English. In fact, only one section, the "About" section, offers the reader an option of reading the text in four languages. These are English, Afrikaans, Sepedi, and Isizulu. There are eleven Constitutionally recognized languages in the nation, so the "About" section offers text in only four of the eleven—only two of the nine African-origin languages.

One might be tempted to interpret these offerings as suggesting that the DA is a regional party. Such a conclusion would be difficult to sustain for two reasons: first, facility in English or Afrikaans is widespread in predominantly African areas that the chosen two African-origin languages do not specifically cater to; second, Sepedi speakers are prevalent in Gauteng, Limpopo, and Mpumalanga, Isizulu speakers are prevalent in KwaZulu-Natal, and thus these two choices cover a large area. They do, however, reflect a northern bias. The nation's southwest is Afrikaans dominated, so it is covered as well. So, the only noticeable gap in the DA's coverage would be the southeast, where Xhosa is dominant. The ANC is especially strong among Xhosa speakers. The relative weakness of the DA in the Xhosa dominated area may well be the reason that the language options for the "About" section seem to exclude the southeast. So, the DA is not signaling that it is regional, just that it is not targeting one section of the nation where it is, for the moment, weak.

The other temptation in analyzing the language choices is to note that Afrikaans, "the language of the oppressor," is prominent. In fact, if one goes to the "Newsroom" section of the website, one finds that subscriptions are available to two DA newsletters, both of which are available only in English and Afrikaans. It might then seem that the DA is making a concerted attempt to attract Afrikaans speakers to the party. Post-1994, Afrikaners were not asked to leave the country; so, there is nothing wrong with either their participation in the nation's civic life or a political party's solicitation of them. In addition, one should note that many non-Afrikaaners in the southwest, especially the nation's colored population, are being arguably solicited through the Afrikaans language option. Still,

Afrikaans seems stressed more than it should be if the DA were simply trying to cover all bases.

The ANC's website offers an interesting contrast. Like the DA's, it is predominantly in English. Only small sections—philosophical ones—are available in other languages; and they are available in all other South African languages, Afrikaans as well as the nine African-origin languages. The contrast suggests that the ANC positions itself nationally whereas the DA positions itself more for some in the nation than for others.

LEADERSHIP

The DA website lists its national leaders, its members in the parliament, and its provincial leaders.

The nine national leaders, a diverse group, should be considered in some detail, since they are the national face of the party. Party leader Helen Zille is promoted on the website as a crusading journalist for the "liberal" *Rand Daily Mail* whose work was responsible for exposing how the police "Special Branch" tortured and murdered activist Steve Biko. Zille eventually turned to politics.

Similarly beyond suspicion would be the two Africans in the group—Lindiwe Mazibuko from the Durban metropolitan area and Mmusi Maimone from the Johannesburg area (specifically Soweto).

In promoting Wilmot James, the DA website stresses his education in the United Kingdom and the United States. In promoting Natashsa Michael, it stresses her immigrant roots (English mother and Italian father).

Dion George attended "Wits," so he is not tainted by a too-Afrikaner education. However, Anchen Dreyer attended Rand Afrikaans and Ivan Myer holds two degrees from Stellenbosch. Their backgrounds are more strikingkly Afrikaner-oriented. And, last, Dianne Kohler Barnard, a journalist from Port Elizabeth, joined politics in protest against ANC interference with the press, something the website says Barnard found similar to NP interference under apartheid.

The group is best described as diverse. If a few tilt in an Afrikaner direction, others, especially Zille, tilt in the opposite. So one might conclude that the leadership group was selected with some attention to the matter of balance.

ETHNIC BALANCE

In assessing balance, one can "eyeball" a group or one can count. With the national leadership, the former approach was taken, for the number under scrutiny was but nine. With the DA's parliamentary delegation, one needs to count. In doing so, one feels guilty of reenacting apartheid era racial categorization; however, if one is to assess whether the DA represents all of the nation's people, there is really no other way than to look at names, pictures, and brief biographies and, then, tally the members by racial category. Doing so, one finds that four may be colored and one is definitely Asian. Of the remaining sixty-five, fifty-five seem white while ten are clearly African.

Recall that earlier a breakdown of 15-5-5-75 was posited as mirroring the nation's white, Asian, colored, African population. The DA's breakdown is (approximately) 79-6-0-14. The DA, then, is clearly far more white than the population and far less black. The names of the white members reveal more: somewhere between half and two-thirds are Afrikaner names.

The provincial leadership picture is similar. Again based on guesses as to ethnicity, the breakdown is 83-0-0-16. Within the white group, Afrikaner names constitute somewhere between half and two-thirds. Also striking in the provincial listing is how 60 percent of the group hails from two of the nation's nine provinces. The listing then suggests that the DA is strongest in the Western Cape, coincidentally an Afrikaner stronghold, with some inroads in the very urban Gauteng. The national and parliamentary listings had suggested that the DA had also made inroads in KwaZulu-Natal, but the provincial numbers suggest that the DA is just as strong—or just as weak—in KwaZulu-Natal as in the ANC-dominated Eastern Cape.

One, of course, does not expect every political party to mirror the nation's ethnic breakdown exactly. In whatever nation one might point to, one will find imbalances. For example, in the United States, both African Americans and Hispanic Americans are underrepresented in the Republican Party. The DA imbalance does, however, point to two important political observations: first, the nation's white population, especially the Afrikaner segment, is flocking to the DA in disproportionate numbers; second, given the nation's history, this disproportion sets the DA up to be, in some observers' view, a political group that might, implicitly or even explicitly, represent retrograde views associated with the apartheid era.

I do need to be very clear here. I am not suggesting that the DA's leadership sees the party as representing views one would associate with the apartheid era National Party. It is clear from the website and from the leaders' public statements that this is not the case. However, the DA's composition may send a message at odds with that of its leadership. If so, there are two explanations one might posit: first, those opposed to or with strong reservations about the change in government in 1994 had to go somewhere and the DA has proven to be the political place; or second, the DA, in the positions it advocates on a range of issues, is offering an appealing agenda to those with reservations, on whatever basis, about the change in government. To test this second explanation, one needs to consider what the DA website says about certain issues.

REDISTRIBUTION OF INCOME AND PROPERTY

At the time of the change in government in 1994, fear of redistribution was widespread among white South Africans. The passage of nearly twenty years would seem to have reduced that fear, for the DA website addresses the issue only implicitly and in passing.

The issue is addressed implicitly in the "Vision" statement's insistence on equality and nondiscrimination based on race. Given this insistence, it is only logical that the DA asks that the path toward progress for the South African people not be determined by demographics. Race is not mentioned but is implicit in the DA's call for "opportunity for the disadvantaged without shutting off opportunity for the advantaged." Doing so might mean, as the DA notes in its "Principles" section, "progressive realization" of the needed advances for the impoverished. The DA, then, implies that change may be slow, not radical as early advocates of redistribution advocated. The DA notes strongly that all South Africans are "legitimate"—in other words, that the tables have not turned, making white South Africans second class and, therefore, subject to any kind of property confiscation. The DA supports its position by citing none other than Nelson Mandela himself, declaring that the land is owned by South Africans black and white.

The DA, then, implicitly rejects redistribution as a strategy while accepting its goals of opportunity for those who had been denied it under apartheid. However, the DA, in the sub-subsection "Land of Opportunity" in the subsection "The Opportunity Society" in the section "Our Policies," admits that "rural land reform" has been inspired by a desire to "redistribute" wealth. The DA does not indict the policy; rather, the DA argues that redistribution should not be the sole rationale and suggests that the land reform process should, perhaps, slow down because the ANC government is providing land but not the services that would permit new owners to make the land productive. One could argue that the DA position is designed to thwart redistribution by citing a reason for slowing it or even stopping it that seems to be very much in the interest of those benefiting from the redistribution policy.

So, in general, the DA in 2012 does not devote a great deal of attention to the redistribution issue, but the party does position itself on the white South Africans' side of the matter. There is even, in the DA's strong indictment of the ANC's complicity in Robert Mugabe's "tyranny" in Zimbabwe (elsewhere under "Our Policies"), a veiled criticism of redistribution since Mugabe stands as an exemplar of redistribution policy.

SOCIAL SERVICES

The DA's insistence on absolute equality would seem from the website to apply to certain categories of social services such as schools, roads, and education. On the services that the disadvantaged need and the advantaged do not, the DA takes the "politically correct" course and insists that the poorest South Africans be served. The DA, however, is vague about how these targeted services might be provided by a government lacking sufficient revenue in a weak economy. In general, the website frequently mentions public-private partnerships as the solution to all ills. Perhaps that is the route the DA would recommend. Or reducing governmental bureaucracy, which is indicted in general and in particular as a barrier to providing adequate public health services.

In one area, however, the DA insists on *not* linking the provision of services to need: a pension for the elderly. All should receive that without the current "needs" test. The DA's position sounds noble, and it sounds as if it is based as much on gratitude as equality. The real basis, however, may be DA's demographics: there are many elderly Afrikaners living in the rural stretches in the Western Cape Province, the only province the DA holds a majority in.

PRIVATE VERSUS PUBLIC

An objective view of the DA's position on redistribution and social services would say it is nuanced insofar as it seems to call for fair treatment for all of the nation's "rainbow people." The position, although critical of the ANC government, does not draw a very well-defined line between the DA position and the ANC position. In general, one might characterized the DA position as more cautious. On the central economic issue facing the nation—who should drive the economy, the private sector or the government, the DA website repeatedly stakes out a position strikingly at odds with what the DA argues the ANC is stressing. Taking a position one might term "libertarian," the DA insists on an individual's economic freedom. Government involvement should be minimal, and, when it exists, it should be provincial or city if at all possible and it should be in close partnership with the private sector whenever possible.

In the website's "About" section, the DA advocates a "devolution of power to locate government as close as possible to the people." Whether close or farther away, the DA declares that the government's role is "to facilitate not direct." Under "Our Policies," the word "direct" is often the stronger "dictate." The ANC's position is argued to be quite different: "In stark contrast, the governing party is increasingly propagating a shift towards a more state-centric interventionist model." The ANC, the DA tells readers, has failed to observe how such a model proved disastrous in both Eastern Europe and elsewhere in Africa.

The nation's schools as well as its public health services must be improved in "partnership with private enterprise." Transportation, more radically, should be privatized, and sport and tourism — heralded as important areas for the country — will require heavy private sector involvement if they are to thrive. Innovation in services as well as innovation throughout the economy depends upon "stronger private sector investment." The ANC is overly interventionist, the DA says; and its intervention is motivated by unspecified reasons other than encouraging growth. Implicit in that DA charge (i.e., in what a cynical reader might think the DA is implying) is either a veiled attack on redistribution or a veiled attack on corruption. Neither of these attacks quite surfaces, but one on bureaucracy and inefficiency does.

CRIME

Somewhat contradictorily, the DA website does support "The right of the people to protection by the state from crime." The DA notes that, in Cape Town, under DA leadership, crime has been reduced but describes the situation throughout the bulk of the country as a "web of terror." To combat the terror, the DA calls for more police as well as a decentralization of the force so that police can better respond to individual communities' needs. The DA also calls for a decrease in police corruption. In keeping with the DA's belief in the private sector, it sees roles for it in not only policing the nation but in accelerating the country's slow-moving judicial processes.

Given that much of the increase in crime has occurred in rural areas, such as the rural Western Cape where the DA is strong, the DA advocates special attention to rural areas and offers many specific recommendations. The DA also advocates more services for victims, including compensation. Given what would be perceived as the DA's special concern for the Afrikaner-dominated rural Western Cape, this call for services and for compensation is, without stating so explicitly, a call for resources to be spent on the nation's minority white population.

If one thinks that there is not a pro-Afrikaner tilt to the DA's website on the issue of crime, one should consider its criticism of the government's decision to phase out the commando system. As South Africans well know, the word "commando" is of Afrikaans origin. It refers to the way, in the very early twentieth century, Afrikaner or Boer farmers would form quasi-military units to engage in some overt and many covert guerilla actions against the British who — lusting for diamonds and gold — were invading the two Afrikaner or Boer states (The Orange Free State and The Transvaal) from the British Cape and Natal colonies. What these commandos did is legendary among Afrikaners. The DA's lament at the phasing out of commandos is, then, not just a way of pointing to a reduced potential law enforcement mechanism in Afrikaner-dominated rural areas but a nod to a celebrated Afrikaner institution and an only slightly veiled critical comment on the ANC's abolition of this Afrikaner tradition.

HIV/AIDS

Early in Thabo Mbeki's presidency, the nation's focus was on its HIV/AIDS epidemic. More recently, the attention has shifted to what might be termed a "co-epidemic" in HIV/AIDS and tuberculosis, with the nation ranking near the top for the incidence of both diseases in global reports. The two are tied together because the immunological deficiencies inherent in AIDS results in the easy acquisition of tuberculosis and severe difficulties in treating it. One might argue that treating tuberculosis without also combatting HIV/AIDS is a losing proposition since the presence of HIV/AIDS makes the prognosis for TB treatment bleak. This "co-epidemic" is certainly one of South Africa's major problems.

The "About" section of the DA website, which reviews the party's "Vision," "Principles," and "History" does not mention either HIV/AIDS or TB. The "Our Policies" section is divided into sub-sections focused on the kind of society the DA wishes to create in South Africa. Thus, it talks about "The Open Society," "The Opportunity Society," "The Caring Society," "The Safe Society," and "The Efficient Society." HIV/AIDS is mentioned first under "The Opportunity Society," in its "Education Policy" sub-subsection. In between discussing the initiatives necessary to help poorer students and proposing that provincial or local schools could opt out of a national curriculum, the website suggests that there should be programs to prevent the loss of teachers to HIV/AIDS. The HIV/AIDS problem seems to have slid in under the backdoor: it is the unfortunate cause of the truly important problem, which is the loss of teachers.

HIV/AIDS does, logically, come up again in the "Caring Society" subsection. HIV/AIDS, in conjunction with TB, is said to be "our major health challenges." However, AIDS is spelled Aids, and the website's limited attention is devoted to discussing TB, not HIV/AIDS.

In passing, HIV/AIDS comes up two more times. In the "Efficient Society" subsection, HIV/Aids (still not spelled as an acronym) and TB are mentioned under "Environment and Energy" because unsanitary environments accelerate the spread of the diseases and under "Public Service Policy" because the ANC-supported bureaucracy, populated by allegedly inept workers, is preventing "an effective AIDS [spelled correctly this time] treatment programme."

The misspelling of AIDS may strike some as trivial—or the result of an unnoticed "spellcheck" correction. However, that misspelling might communicate to the part of the population ravaged by the disease—much more African than white; heavily in KwaZulu-Natal if tuberculosis is coupled with HIV/AIDS—that the DA is not as knowledgeable or concerned about the issue as it should be. The misspelling, combined with the small amount of attention paid to the issue, might communicate that it is, as far as the DA is concerned, one that affects a constituency other than its primary ones as defined by race and region.

CONCLUSION

An opposition party is, of course, not expected to agree with the party in power. So, of course there are differences between the DA and the ANC. Given South Africa's political history, an opposition party must exercise care in establishing those differences. The opposition party must make sure it is committed to the principles that define post-apartheid South Africa while both taking issue with the ANC government and defending a philosophy of government that is quite different from that of the ANC. Should the support of the principles seem lukewarm and should the oppositional stance seem strident, the DA runs the risk of being perceived as retrograde by some in and some out of South Africa.

Let me very clear: I am not suggesting that the present-day DA is a revival of the National Party of the 1950s, 1960s, and 1970s that, first, erected the laws and structures of apartheid and, then, enforced them with an oppressive police presence. Although there are certainly many South Africans who still adhere to the racist views of these earlier decades, the DA's leadership has clearly put these earlier times behind them. They make it very clear at the party website that they have embraced the themes of Mandela's initial ANC government—diversity, equality, reconciliation.

The question, then, is not about the DA but about the rhetoric of the DA and whether it has handled well the difficult exigence outlined above. My argument is that it has not.

First, although the principles defining a post-apartheid South Africa are clearly embraced, they are quickly turned to the DA's political advantage. Equality is used as a tool to slow down if not thwart any attempt at either property or income redistribution or radical changes in how social services are provided. Implicit in the DA's words are a challenge to the ANC government to act in accordance with the belief in equality for all and with Mandela's stated position that South Africa belongs to all of its rainbow peoples. What the DA implicitly rejects is anything resembling what in this country we would term "affirmative action" for those long-oppressed and long-disadvantaged by the former white racist state.

Second, although the DA is of course free to raise the issues that concern its constituencies and to pay less attention to the issues that are of less concern, the DA's website pushes a bit too far in both its advocating and its ignoring. The party is right to raise the issue of crime, especially in rural areas; however, the party did not have to bring up the matter of discontinued commando forces. The party, perhaps, can downplay the HIV/AIDS and tuberculosis "co-epidemic" somewhat; however, more should be said, what is said shouldn't come across as either incidental (e.g., a reason for the loss of talented school teachers), or an excuse for an attack on the ANC (e.g., an example of the bureaucracy's failure). And AIDS should be spelled correctly, so that a reader of the website is not left wondering if the DA knows it's an acronym and knows what the four letters stand for.

Third, although the DA will, of course, take potshots at the ANC—after all, it is politics, the DA should not do so in a manner that evokes racist stereotypes. When criticizing the state-centric philosophy of the ANC and the resulting bureaucracy, the DA reminds readers of the failure of that philosophy elsewhere in Africa. Thus, the DA—inadvertently, I would assume—evokes the stereotypical picture of black-led postcolonial governments that were notorious for inefficiency and corruption. The DA, then, may be suggesting to some that it views the ANC government is falling into this pattern. When discussing the nation's foreign affairs, the DA reminds readers of what it presents, vaguely, as the ANC government's complicity with Robert Mugabe's government in Zimbabwe. The ANC would undoubtedly present its involvement with Mugabe as representing an attempt to evoke pro-democratic reforms from within Zimbabwe. The DA's website, because it is vague and because it uses the word "complicity," suggests that the ANC involvement has been in support of such policies as property confiscation and the violent, anti-democratic suppression of one's political opposition. Is the DA suggesting that the ANC in South Africa might follow Mugabe's example? Probably not, but it is worth noting that, in introducing DA leader Dianne Kohler Barnard, the website notes that she gave up on journalism because she was experiencing interference from the ANC government reminiscent of NP interference with press freedom under apartheid. There then seems to be implicit in spots on the website the fear that the ANC might move in an anti-democratic direction either like the NP's or like Mugabe's.

Fourth, although the DA can, of course, advocate a governmental philosophy quite different from that espoused by the ANC, the DA's advocacy could easily be seen as supporting structures that undergirded white—more specifically, Afrikaner—power in South Africa. The advocacy of provincial and local power over national power opens up the possibility of a nonuniform march away from the vestiges of apartheid. In talking about educational policy, for example, the DA website argues for communities and, within reason, parents having the right to choose the primary language of instruction in their schools. If such a policy were to be followed, then there would be Afrikaans language schools in some of the parts of South Africa where the DA is strongest. Now this possibility may strike a non-South African reader as a good thing: a community's language being respected. However, one needs to contextualize what may well be a veiled call for Afrikaans language school in the nation's historical context. In that context, Afrikaans was the language of the oppressor, and hundreds of schoolchildren were murdered when they demonstrated against its preeminence in the schools. Certainly the possibility that a small school in the rural Western Cape might have an Afrikaans language school is not the same things as Afrikaans language schools in Soweto. Still, what the DA points to when it operationalizes its call for a weak central government under "Educational Policy" disturbingly evokes the pre-1994 period. Local or even provincial power then might be a tool that could take at least some pockets in the nation back to an earlier time.

The DA governmental philosophy also puts the private sector over the public. As the DA presents recent political history on its website, the ANC has led South Africa in a state-centric direction. The DA wants then to reverse this trend and, arguably, return to the way the private-public balance was. Under apartheid, the private sector was white, a mix of Anglophone and Afrikaans-speaking. Since apartheid crumbled, the private sector has become more ethnically diverse. Still, there is a white private sector presence that far exceeds the white presence in the population. Therefore, the DA's stress on the private sector is a stress on a sector where white South Africans still are very present. The structures that the private sector set up—banks and the like—did indeed support an apartheid society between the early 1950s and the late 1980s. So reversing the ANC direction is not just a return to more white presence but also a return to some of the structures associated in many minds with the pre-1994 regime.

These four reasons focus on what the DA website says about various public policies. On four counts, the DA is saying things that could, in some minds, label the party retrograde. One must, however, put these policy statements in the demographic context set up by the DA's website when it presents who its leaders are. Although the national leadership team exhibits diversity, the entire team seems disproportionately white and strikingly Afrikaner. It is, of course, not required that a political party mirror the demographics of a nation. American political parties certainly do not do that: African Americans, for example, are disproportionately represented by the Democratic Party and under-represented in the Republican. However, when there is a disproportion—especially a dramatic disproportion—it is a matter of note and of concern. In this case, the concern is that the DA looks too much like the apartheid era white government. The reader knows it is not, and the reader can of course see the scattered nonwhite faces. Nonetheless, the DA does not look like "the rainbow nation" as much as it looks like the NP of old. In the context provided by this picture, the DA's policy positions gain even more of a retrograde feel.

This analysis—I must stress—is not of the DA, but of the DA as it communicates itself through its website. If one were to have a conversation with members individually or even meet with a group, once might conclude that it was a forward-looking party with some sharp philosophical differences with the ANC. One might further conclude that the existence of these differences was good for the nation: they would prompt debate, and debate would produce better policymaking. If one were, in other words, to consider other DA communication, one might not feel uneasy about the party's role in post-apartheid South Africa. However, based on a close consideration of just the website, a piece of communication the DA composes to present itself, there is cause for concern.

The political concern is that the DA might really be a retrograde group or even a safe haven for the Afrikaners who ruled the roost between 1948 and 1994. Whether there is any basis for that concern I leave for South Africans to decide. As a rhetorician, my argument is that the DA website was a response to an exigence and that those who composed the website did not respond very effectively to that exigence. They came close to sending the opposite message to the one they needed to send to position themselves as a positive, productive "loyal opposition" in the "New South Africa."

NOTE

1. For a discussion of Mbeki's rhetoric in HIV/AIDS, see my article "The Rhetoric of Thabo Mbeki on HIV/AIDS: Strategic Scapegoating?" in the *Howard Journal of Communications* 15.2 (2004): 69–82.

TEN

Responding to Being Sacked

Gough Whitlam on November 11, 1975

This chapter focuses on a strikingly memorable moment in November 1975. After a political crisis lasting approximately a month, Australia was thrown into a constitutional crisis on November's eleventh day. This chapter will, ultimately, read outgoing Prime Minister Edward Gough Whitlam's speech as he left office that afternoon. It is a fascinating speech because of how it managed to maintain a balance between bitter anger and dutiful restraint. To understand the moment and the speech, an American audience needs political background. Fortunately, although the name Gough Whitlam is not familiar to very many Americans, the situation strangely is.

BACKGROUND

During the Clinton presidency, there were tense moments when the government was at the point of shutting down. Such moments have also occurred during the Obama presidency. During both administrations, a budget was necessary to carry on, but the opposition was refusing to pass the budget—in either a firm or a temporary form—until the Democratic administration and Democratic legislators were willing to agree to other measures. These moments have been chronicled in the media as "show-downs"; perhaps they have been "hyped." Realistically, what harm would several days shut-down do, especially since there are safety valves aplenty that would keep some government operations going even "without supply." Both parties have joined in the "hype," ready to accuse the other of the horrors of shutting down the government. During the Clinton administration, the president decided to call House Speaker Newt Gingrich's bluff. Clinton let the government shut down and succeeded in painting Gingrich and the Republicans as the villains. Clinton, arguably a weakened president because of legislative failures, began his latest comeback in the wake of this shut down. Obama has thus far preferred negotiating to calling the house speaker's bluff.

The situation in Australia in fall 1975 was comparable. Whitlam's Labor Party had ruled Australia for several years. As of late, a combination of scandals and unpopular decisions and probably Labor Party complacency had led to Liberal Party upsurge. (One should note that the Liberal Party in Australia defines "Liberal" differently than we do in the United States. We would consider the Australian Liberal Party to be "Conservative." Whitlam's Liberal successor, John Malcolm Fraser, would be seen by Americans as in the mode of Ronald Reagan or Margaret Thatcher.) The resurgent Liberals decided to make the Whitlam budget into an issue that would bring down the government by forcing an election.

The Liberals did not succeed in the House, but a coalition with another party the Liberals had formed was able to block passage in the Senate. Railing against the Senate, implying that it was not serving the people and implying that it was stretching the procedures of governing to the point that they violated the spirit (at least) of the constitution, Whitlam was gradually making political progress against this coalition. Much has been written on these months in Australian political history, and commentators disagree as to whether the coalition was crumbling or not as November 11 approached.[1] Some political figures, thought to be wavering then, said afterward that they were not wavering at all. Of course, it is easy to say that afterward.

So far, the story sounds as if it could happen in the United States. The quirk in the Australian story is the result of two constitutional differences: first, Australia had a parliamentary system of government; second, Australia is not yet a Republic but still part of the British Commonwealth. The first difference means that party leaders, after elections in which they have gained a majority in the House, form the government with the party leader becoming the Prime Minister and other party members acquiring the portfolios of other ministries. The second difference means that these party leaders must ask the permission of "The Crown"—that is, the King or Queen of England—to form a government. A corollary to the second difference is that "The Crown" can dismiss both the government and dissolve the parliament should it care to. Since the King or Queen are quite remote, their royal power is exercised by the Governor General.

If one were to look at Australian currency, one would find Elizabeth II on both coins and bills. This serves as a hint to visitors that there is a British connection, but visitors might well dismiss the British presence as "history." Well, it's not. Despite several referenda to renounce the British tie and become a Republic, Australia has maintained its loyalty to "The

Crown." But Australians and Brits alike understand that the tie is more symbolic than real. At the time of World War I, the tie was still quite real, as thousands of young Australians fought valiantly for distant England. During World War II, Australia had its own threat to contend with to its north—Japan, thereby limiting its ability to help the "Mother Country." And, beginning with World War II and progressing through various the "police actions" of the post-1950 decades, the political tie has probably been stronger with the United States than with the United Kingdom. Still, the tie technically exists.

That it "technically" exists means that "The Crown," of course, consents to a government's formation and that "The Crown," of course, would never use its power to dismiss or dissolve. Thus, in 1975, many Australians were shocked when Governor General John Kerr did indeed use this power. Whitlam, in hindsight, was probably a poor reader of Kerr in their many meetings, for all reports suggest that Whitlam was shocked when, in the late morning of November 11, Kerr summoned Whitlam to the Governor General's study and dismissed the prime minister.

Arguably in shock, Whitlam went home, had a thick steak for lunch, and, then, gradually began sharing the news that the Labor government had been "sacked." For a period, rumors flew, but, during this period, ministers kept at their jobs, almost laughing at the very notion that the Governor General had used his constitutional power and dismissed them. Early in the afternoon, Labor Senators did not know that Whitlam's government had been dismissed when they voted for a compromise that provided the necessary "supply." They thought that Whitlam, behind the scenes, had orchestrated the compromise when the truth was that Liberal Party leader Fraser had. So, within hours of Whitlam's dismissal and Fraser's elevation by Kerr, Fraser had delivered a budget, something Whitlam had not been able to do for months. At this point, Fraser went public, announcing that he was indeed the new prime minister.

Although Whitlam himself had been arguably slow to respond, the Labor Party tried to act quickly. Some argued that Labor should refuse to be dismissed, that Labor should defy "The Crown." If Labor had done so, their action would have transformed a surprising enactment of constitutional provisions into a true constitutional crisis. There were whispers among Labor leaders about who had control of the military along with rumors—probably more than that—that the Governor General had secured control. Thus, the constitutional crisis might well have led to Kerr ordering the Australian military (or, perhaps, just police) to physically remove the Labor ministers from office. Furthermore, there were rumors that many Australian military and police would have refused an order emanating from "The Crown." Such a refusal would have very much fit the anti-authoritarian Aussie culture. It is doubtful that shots would have been fired, but, had Labor provoked a crisis, there almost certainly would have soon been another referendum on a republic. This one would likely not have failed out of sentimentality or concern about the technical details of a republic: the Governor General's actions had produced sufficient resentment on the part of everyday Australians who wondered if Kerr had failed to understand that his powers existed but were not to be used.

Labor decided to fight back through a "no confidence" vote in the new Fraser government. However, by the time the House passed the measure, Fraser had secured supply in the Senate. Kerr then could declare the "no confidence" vote irrelevant and dissolve the entire parliament. Late afternoon on the eleventh, he did so. Labor politicians were incensed—angry at Kerr and Fraser and also not entirely happy with Whitlam who many thought had moved too slowly in response to the moves Kerr and Fraser were making. Whitlam was also incensed but also personally affronted. Whitlam was probably still somewhat in shock, for, in hours, he had fallen from prime minister at the top of the government to, at best, the future leader of the opposition, should Labor choose to keep him at its helm.

The events and the dynamics on that November 11 have been studied at length by both historians and political scientists. The rendition I offered does not do either the history or the political complexities of the situation justice. My goal, however, is not to talk about either the history or the politics per se, but to study the communication event that culminated the afternoon: Gough Whitlam's extemporaneous speech as he left the parliament building in Canberra. It is perhaps the most remembered speech in Australian political history. Words spoken in Australia since have certainly had more profound resonance through the country—the words of the High Court in its *Mabo* decisions which restored land rights to aboriginals and the legislature's apology to the "Stolen Generations" orchestrated by the Kevin Rudd Labor government at its onset. But when asked about speeches per se, Australians are likely to recall Whitlam's November 11, 1975, speech in the same way Americans recall John F. Kennedy's 1961 inaugural or even Dr. Martin Luther King Jr.'s 1963 "I Have a Dream" speech delivered before the Lincoln Memorial.

THE SPEECH

The brief speech will be considered from three perspectives: its exigencies and how it responded to them; its short-term and long-term effects; and why it is so fondly—even passionately—remembered despite its very limited long-term effect.

Its Exigencies

Whitlam's exigencies, then, as he speaks on the steps of the Canberra Parliament building late in the afternoon are complex. He wants to present Governor General Kerr in a negative light, but he does not want to criticize the Queen whom Kerr represents; he wants to present Fraser in a negative light as well, perhaps more so because Whitlam will presumably lead Labor in the forthcoming election against Fraser and the Liberals; and he wants to sustain the anger being shown in and outside the parliament and transform it into a strong anti-Liberal vote. Finally, he wants to come across as in charge, contrary to the impression he may have given at moments during the dramatic and difficult day.

The dissolution proclamation read in the House that afternoon ended ritualistically with "God save the Queen." Whitlam begins his speech by declaring that nobody, not even God, can save John Kerr.[2] What he did that day was beyond forgiveness. But what had he done? Whitlam does not answer that question. Instead, he allows his audience to fill in the blank. That blank is probably filled in with something like "affronted Australian political independence" by many. And that is precisely how Whitlam wanted the people to view Kerr's actions. If Whitlam had addressed the specifics of Kerr's actions, the Labor leader would have had to admit that Kerr acted constitutionally, even if without precedent. That admission would have inevitably raised the question as to why Kerr acted as he did, and those answering the question would have had to consider Kerr's view that Whitlam was incapable of governing because he could not bring in a supply bill. Whitlam, of course, does not want the matter of his capability to be even raised.

Whitlam would prefer for the incident to be understood by his Australian audience in terms of "style." Whitlam—and Labor—believed in a popular approach. Matters of governance should be discussed by the elected representatives of the people—in public fora as well as the one-on-one and small group gatherings common in practical politics. Matters handled in this manner sometimes would take time to be resolved, but they would be by the people's agents. Kerr—Whitlam would have his audience believe—favored a less raucous politics, characterized by not only many private conversations but also some secret ones. Kerr's style, then, was opposed to Whitlam's; and Whitlam would like his audience to believe that Kerr sacked him because of "style," not substance.

Vagueness, then, was Whitlam's ally in his address. It allowed his auditors to fill in blanks in ways that favored his cause. It also allowed Whitlam to avoid dragging the Queen into the matter at all. As he presented what has transpired on the eleventh, the unforgivable actions were entirely Kerr's. The constitutional fact that Kerr represented the monarch was not mentioned. Reporters, however, are not likely to ignore the fact that Kerr was Queen Elizabeth II's agent. So, in the quick inter-

view that followed the speech, a reporter asked Whitlam whether Kerr
had consulted Buckingham Palace and, implicitly, was following the
Queen's orders. Whitlam's response was curious. Certainly not knowing
one way or the other if Elizabeth had been consulted, Whitlam declared
that, of course, Buckingham Palace had not been.[3] His use of metono-
my—saying "Buckingham Palace" as a stand-in for the Queen—allowed
Whitlam to deny any involvement by the British government in the dismissal or dissolution. This denial is based on Whitlam's presumption, but
that presumption served him well in this case, for it allowed him to
present the political confrontation in terms that did not involve "The
Crown." His quick rejection of the very notion of British involvement is
also telling.

Australian attitudes toward "The Crown" are complex—and perhaps
irrational. Australia certainly has many reasons to renounce "The
Crown," foremost the fact that, although Australia came to the defense of
the "Mother Country" in World War I, the "Mother Country" had proven
unable to come to the defense of Australia in World War II. Thus, Australia had moved into the American orbit, making the Australia-United
Kingdom link a political anachronism. In addition, in the years since
settlement and confederation, Australia had grown apart from the United
Kingdom, increasingly positioning itself as not only a Pacific country but
an Asian one. Still, at a deep level, there was still an allegiance to Great
Britain that had some people still using the word "home" to refer to the
United Kingdom, not to Australia. Given this allegiance, a feeling that
probably transcended party labels, Whitlam did not want to indict "The
Crown" for what had transpired on November 11. Certainly some pro-
Republic voices would have cheered a Whitlam indictment of "The
Crown," but it would probably have alienated as many people as it
pleased. More important, such an indictment would raise an irrelevant
issue, for it was to the conspiracy between Kerr and Fraser that Whitlam
wanted to point.

In the speech, Whitlam runs the risk of boring his audience as he
reviews the documents issued that day. He reviews them because he
wants to establish that Malcolm Fraser, the Liberal Party leader, was
involved in the events long before he stood up in the House and declared
that he was now prime minister. In other words, Whitlam wants to establish that Kerr and Fraser were involved in a conspiracy. Convinced that
Fraser could bring in a supply bill, Kerr commissioned him as head of
government and then let him keep the matter a secret until he could
secure a favorable Senate vote for supply. That all of this was done in
secret is what Whitlam wants his audience to understand. Whereas Labor
operated in a public manner, Kerr and Fraser were conspiring in a private
one. Whitlam implies that such a way of proceeding was not very Australian.

After November 11, 1975, Whitlam has no communication whatsoever with Kerr—probably by Whitlam's choice. But Whitlam would have to deal with Fraser, either as opposition leader in a Fraser government or as prime minister with Fraser leading the Liberal opposition. It is therefore somewhat surprising then that Whitlam exercised his sharp wit and referred as Fraser as "Kerr's cur" in the speech. The phrase, of course, attracted media attention, and it was a long time before Malcolm Fraser overcame the sobriquet. The phrase, however, did more than reduce Fraser to a dog, for it also reduced him to being subordinate to—even in service of—Kerr. If God could not save John Kerr, what then—one might ask—would be the fate of the man who "fetched" a supply bill from the Senate under false pretenses at John Kerr's command? Whitlam positions Fraser in such a way that he scarcely seems prime ministerial material.

Whitlam's speech does not address his steak luncheon; nor does it mention anything Whitlam did or said during the course on November 11. When the proclamation dissolving parliament was read, there were raucous "We want Gough" chants almost drowning the proclamation out. These came not from a gallery but from the House floor. (Legislatures outside the United States are often raucous to a degree that surprises American observers.) These chants suggested that Whitlam still had a great deal of Labor Party support. However, there were also some in the party who were questioning the quality of his leadership. On that day, in these members' opinion, he had not led. Rather, he had sat back and let the events unfold. His stopping to eat the steak for lunch galled these members: Whitlam should have been rallying the troops, perhaps organizing defiance against Kerr's unprecedented order, not relaxing over a good meal. So, the chants may have been half-hearted on the parts of even some who were trying to drown out the odious proclamation from Kerr.

Whitlam's words that afternoon did little to overcome this discontent. But his manner might have accomplished what words did not. He was not cowed; rather, he was defiant. He damned Kerr; he maligned Fraser; he meticulously pointed out proof of a Kerr-Fraser conspiracy. The text of Whitlam's speech is difficult to come by, probably because it was extemporaneous. One who wants to study the speech is almost forced to go to the audio versions that exist—partial in the ABC (Australian Broadcasting Corporation) archives; full in the SoundScreen archives. These audio versions make Whitlam's spirited delivery clear: he speaks like a leader, not a broken man. If one adds the audiotape of the post-speech interview to the speech, the picture becomes one of a spirited leader when called upon to address the growing crowd but a more restrained statesman leader when asked questions by reporters intent upon getting a "good quote" or a dramatic headline.

Whitlam's manner of delivering the speech also undoubtedly inspired both the pro-Labor crowd that had gathered and pro-Labor auditors throughout the country. He did more, however, than just count on his spirit. He told his auditors that they needed to sustain the energy evident in their enthusiastic support of him for the months ahead. The Labor government had been silenced, Whitlam told his auditors, presumably by the Kerr-Fraser conspiracy, but Labor voters could not be—in the months ahead and at the next polling.

All in all, the address responded to the exigencies very well. Whitlam managed to put both Kerr and Fraser in unflattering lights, while not confronting "The Crown" at all. Whitlam was strategically vague, allowing him to paint Kerr and Fraser as villains, himself as victim, and the Queen as not involved. Furthermore, he came across as strong—angry, yes, but in a restrained manner befitting one who would lead the country. This strength plus his words saluting the crowd's enthusiasm helped him initiate the Labor Party's campaign that very afternoon. As its initiator and as its cheerleader, he would be difficult to replace at the head even if some in Labor might want to.

Effects

The speech walked a tightrope: it was angry enough insofar as it situated Kerr among the unredeemed and labeled Fraser as "Kerr's cur" that it rallied Labor support and got media attention, but it was not a call for defiance. Labor would abide by Kerr's decisions, as offensive to Australian political independence as they might be. The battle would not be there at the parliament house but in the forthcoming election of a new House, a new Senate, and a new government. Whitlam's speech was sufficiently rallying that Labor ended the day convinced that they could hold the House and gain the Senate, that the new government would be the old Whitlam one, Kerr and Fraser be damned. By all accounts then, the speech was, in the short term, a success.

Labor, however, would lose the election—by a large margin. One is therefore tempted to label Whitlam's speech a long-term failure. It rallied Labor, but only for the moment. The truth, however, may be that no speech could have saved Labor from a combination of its own errors, its over-reaching when it came to both reform and the expansion of government services, and international economic circumstances. Whitlam had pushed forward an ambitious agenda, but he had not kept very tight reins on his ministers, some of whom had pursued misguided courses. His popular politicking style had offended Kerr; his delegating and trusting style had produced one questioning headline after another. His beliefs had made him a political hero for many on the left, but his manner of governing had convinced Kerr that he lacked the necessary tact and many in the nation that he lacked the necessary control.

Meanwhile, the global economy saw many developed nations suffering from high inflation and high unemployment. Then, oil prices shot up as many OPEC nations retaliated economically against supporters of Israel by reducing production. Australia was affected less than most, but, still, the nation found itself in a precarious global economic context that seemed to counsel caution in public policy, not the sometimes breakneck-speed reform and public sector growth Whitlam pushed. There was then a gut-level reaction against the Labor agenda that Whitlam was largely powerless to stop. Before the crisis of fall 1975, political observers knew as much. In fact, that reaction was fueling the Senate opposition to the Whitlam budget. The National Party–Liberal Party coalition there that held a majority was trying to force Labor to call an election to get a budget through. The coalition sensed that it could make a proverbial killing in an election. Although Whitlam's speech on November 11 may well have improved Labor's chances, the odds were still very much against Whitlam's party. The speech then may have been a long-term failure not because it was rhetorically inept but because majority sentiment in the nation had turned in a more cautious directions. It was not that the public saw Whitlam as reckless; rather, they saw him as a fiery spirit at a time when greater restraint was necessary. Thus, the speech may actually have hurt his cause for it confirmed, in neutral eyes, that fiery spirit even though it carefully stayed on the "correct" side of the compliant-defiant line.

An assessment of Whitlam's speech, then, must acknowledge that it was not, ultimately, a success if success is to be measured by the fate of the Labor Party in the upcoming election. That is, of course, not the only measure that is possible; and one can argue that no speech could have reversed the downward spiral Labor was in. So, perhaps a better assessment should be based on how well the speech responded to the exigencies Whitlam faced and how the speech gave Labor a momentary spark. So, I think one can conclude that the speech was somewhat successful, but "somewhat successful" does not seem to fit a speech that is lauded as one of the most significant, most memorable in Australian history.

The Speech as Australian

Its being memorable and significant may, of course, be connected to how unusual and thus memorable the occasioning event was, but I don't think those who laud the speech have simply the occasion in mind. They are pointing to some quality that makes the speech significant that has nothing to do with whether it was extremely successful or not. That quality is its ability to evoke the national identity.

Consider a successful and significant American speech for a minute: Franklin Delano Roosevelt's 1933 inaugural. Roosevelt responded well to the speech's particular exigencies: he calmed fears; he rallied the people against the villain they needed to blame their economic hardship on. FDR also delivered the address well, using his eloquent "radio voice." But, read years later, the speech is no masterpiece: it ranks well below Lincoln's second inaugural and Kennedy's not only in beauty but in other qualities both aesthetic and political. The strength of the Roosevelt address is that it tapped into two American identities—as not giving way in the face of fear, as not letting the powerful suppress the people. We are as fearless as our pioneering forefathers; we are as much "the people" as those forefathers who rebelled against the powerful British and resented the touches of aristocracy that popped up in post-Revolution America. FDR evoked this "we," and his auditors cheered his characterization of Americans as much as if not more than his specific messages.

Whitlam's speech evokes what it means to be an Australian in the same manner as Roosevelt's evokes what it means to be an American. So, what does it mean to be an Australian?

This is an often studied question. Early answers—termed "classic" by those who concur—offered stereotypes that were partially true.[4] Later answers qualified the stereotypes, leading to a more balanced (i.e., not as rural) picture. Then, as waves of immigrants came to Australia, the picture became much more multicultural, although, even in the present-day multicultural Australia there persists a national identity shared by many. In 1975, that identity was undoubtedly somewhat stronger.

The identity has many facets. A "mateship" born of rural work together is part of it, as is the courage and fatalism born in the experience of the "diggers" in World War I. Even more basic is Australia's origin as a penal colony. For a long time, one's convict roots were to be hidden; later, they were to be celebrated. But in the open or not, these roots fueled a resentment of authority. The national character then is irreverent, and the frequent targets of the irreverence are those who act in a manner "too British." This irreverence usually stopped just short of rebellion: the typical Australian would let authorities know just how he or she felt before, drink in hand, complying with dictates. This typical Australian also believed in a "fair go" and in the people, particularly ordinary people, as what mattered.

Whitlam's brief speech embodied this Australian identity. It began with memorable irreverence—saying that God wouldn't save John Kerr, labeling Fraser "Kerr's cur." Kerr was tainted by his British role; Fraser by his association with the very proper Kerr. Whitlam's irreverence, then, although not directed against the United Kingdom, had an anti-British feel.

Although some had advocated defiance and although many who had gathered in Canberra that afternoon might have cheered it and defied authority in their own way through strikes and the like, Whitlam stopped just short of rebellion. He had no drink in hand, but one can almost imagine he had as he lambasted Kerr and Fraser and asked the crowd to sustain their anger through to the upcoming elections. There would be no defiance that day; there would be no strikes the next; but there would be defiance shown through a pro-Labor vote a month hence.

Whitlam also was so very Australian in his scathing discussion of how Kerr and Fraser had proceeded. Their actions were not above-board: they made deals, they kept secrets, they manipulated both people and the constitution. In their political world, a "fair go" was not valued. Loyal, hard-working ministers were to be dismissed; elected officials were to be kept in the dark. This was not the way a government that valued a "fair go" operated. The typical Australian valued a government in which the people's representatives were at the fore, especially in the House where representation was constitutionally stronger. The House had voted "no confidence" in the Liberals; the House had asked Kerr to turn back to Whitlam and away from Fraser, but Kerr had dismissed the House action as irrelevant in the face of dissolution. A backroom (well, actually study) deal had thwarted the people; so had the dissolution.

Whitlam, then, embodied the Australian identity in his speech by being irreverent, by defying authority to a point, by insisting on a politics characterized by both fair play and the people's voice. He became everybody's "battler," everybody's "mate." The speech, then, is memorable and significant not because of the on-the-fly rhetorical skill it exhibited but because of the persona Whitlam exhibited. He projected himself as an Australian, not challenging "The Crown" per se, but challenging an action that, in some unarticulated way, his auditors saw as oozing with British authority. He stood for Australia, irreverently rejecting the colonial authority that, in the constitution but beyond the pale, still stood and a governing style that was not in line with Australia's image of itself.

Very few Australian prime ministers are famous. Somewhat surprisingly, the ones who are tend to be subjects of continuing controversy. To this day, in some eyes, Gough Whitlam is a hero tragically cut down in his prime. He was a crusader for all causes that we in the United States would term "liberal." He reduced Australian involvement in the conflict in Vietnam, he tried to extend rights to groups in Australia that had been denied them, and he tried to extend government services at a low (or no) cost to many who needed them. He was also a reformist, who saw many ways in which Australia had not kept up with progressive governments like the United States and Europe; and, as such, he was determined to bring Australia into the present day in terms of government-provided services. In other eyes, however, Whitlam was not only too much an advocate of government involvement and objectionable on philosophical grounds but too much a delegator who could not control the others in his government. This inability to control was also seen, critics would argue, in his problems marshaling the legislature.

Whether seen as a crusader or an incompetent, that afternoon on November 11, he came across as neither of these but, instead, as an Aussie, rhetorically defying the high-handedness of dismissal and dissolution and defending fair play and the people's will. For a short moment, he was iconic. Although he eventually lost, his very Australian speech that afternoon probably did guarantee one outcome he would most certainly applaud: it is highly unlikely a Governor General will ever exercise his or her constitutional authority again and dismiss the government. Henceforth, it is quite likely that the Governor General will sit more on the political sidelines, acting as the Australian psyche wants him or her to act.

NOTES

1. See for example the account of Whitlam's term in Grattan's *Australian Prime Ministers* also see the broader discussion in Macintyre's *A Concise History of Australia.*

2. A copy of this speech is difficult to locate, but a recorded version is available through the National Film and Screen Archives in Canberra and online.

3. For the text of this press conference, see www.whittendismissal.com/1975/11/11/ whitten-post-dismissal-press-conference.htm.

4. The classic formulation of the Australian character is Russell Ward's in *The Australian Legend.*

ELEVEN

The Political Dimension of the Statesman's Farewell

The Case of Australia's Kevin Rudd

As already noted when dealing with Mwai Kibaki's speeches in Kenya, one important body of political communication scholarship deals with genre. Karlyn Kohrs Campbell and Kathleen Hall Jamieson in *Deeds Done in Words* (1990) defined several presidential genres. Then, they updated that work in *Presidents Creating the Presidency* (2008). Others have explored other genres that rhetors other than presidents occasionally use such as the apology and the commemoration. Certainly, some of these political genres have analogues abroad. Again, as noted in chapter 6, considering them critically advances our understanding of political communication in two inversely related ways. First, examining texts from abroad using the lens of existing American genres may alert scholars to dimensions of those texts that they otherwise might not adequately note. Second, examining these texts with an eye to how they depart from the American definition may alert scholars to further rhetorical possibilities for the genre under consideration. In other words, the genre's definition might become broader if non-American uses are examined.

This chapter enacts that back-and-forth process with the genre of the farewell. As Campbell and Jamieson note, some—far from all—presidents, beginning, of course, with George Washington, have chosen to offer final words to the American people. Although the genre thereby defined may not be as rigid as others, such as the inaugural, with more exemplars, nonetheless, the genre of farewell can be said to exhibit four traits. First, it enacts an important national ritual of power-passing insofar as the sitting president signals his transition from president to just citizen. Second, it does so in a solemn tone befitting a ritualistic moment. Third, it sums up, almost always in positive terms, the accomplishments of the outgoing administration. Fourth, it offers counsel, conventionally in the form of warnings.

In the United States, the genre is tied to the four-year election cycle. Should a farewell be delivered, its timing is predictable. Only in the case of Richard M. Nixon, who resigned the presidency and therefore left office at an unpredicted moment, do we have a departure from the norm. And most would probably not consider Nixon's farewell speech to be a "true" farewell, given the circumstances under which it was given. In fact, Nixon may well be argued to have given two farewell addresses — the speech in which he announces that he will resign and the speech in which he takes leave. Considering these as farewells would compel a slight rethinking of the genre since they have an exigence somewhat different from the norm. Such a rethinking might be in order, as the analysis of an international example suggests.

In the international arena, leave-taking by the national chief executive is not as predictable and regularized as in the United States. Leaving the matter of coup d'etats aside, even in a parliamentary system, the prime minister in power may lose confidence — of the legislative body, of a governor general (should there be one), or of the party he or she heads. The situation is more volatile; the leave-taking, more wrapped in political controversy. The situation might be more like the one that faced Nixon than the one that has faced every other outgoing president.

The farewell address offered by outgoing Australia Prime Minister Kevin Rudd on June 14, 2010, suggests how the international arena may see the genre used differently than in almost all American instances. This chapter offers background necessary to understand Rudd's farewell, examines the speech rhetorically, and reflects on how, thanks to the example of Rudd's address, we should see the farewell genre as potentially far more political than it seems at first glance.

BACKGROUND

John Howard's term as prime minister began as a strong conservative reaction to the policies of the Labor government led by Paul Keating. The term was also a reaction against Keating's sometimes imperious style. The Howard government, however, became vulnerable after September 11, 2001, because many Australians saw Howard as sycophantic toward George W. Bush and had tired of Australia's involvement in the American president's military actions. The Howard government was also vulnerable because it was being challenged on the right by Pauline Hanson's "One Nation" party, which had considerable following in the state of Queensland. Howard's party (the conservative-oriented party known in Australian as the Liberal Party) won reelection in 2004 because Howard's strong anti-immigration stance had rallied his conservative supporters and Labor leader Mark Latham's personal behavior had raised concerns about how well he might govern. Howard was not, however, as lucky in 2007, when Rudd led Labor to a parliamentary majority.

Rudd began Labor's term by charismatically pushing for an official apology to the nation's aboriginal people and by shrewdly pushing for greater economic ties with Asia. However, several characteristics of Rudd's governance increasingly made him weaker and more vulnerable. He was seen by some as too pro-Asian, to the point where he was thought to be too often in Asia (and too often speaking Mandarin Chinese) and not often enough in Australia, tending to home affairs. He often brought both emotion and religion into government, causing some to view him as not always governing by reason; and he sometimes governed without observing adequately the niceties of parliamentary rule and party protocol. He was, in other words, too often a "lone ranger" politician in some eyes. These traits made him vulnerable and, thus, Labor vulnerable. The result was his replacement as leader of the Labor Party—and, thus, prime minister—by Julia Gillard. His speech, then, is his farewell as prime minister—not because his party lost an election but because his party lost confidence in him as its leader.

RUDD'S FAREWELL

Rudd's address is strikingly casual and personal.[1] It is, thus, not the ritualistic farewell American leaders offer. He notes the transition that is occurring, but his leave-taking lacks the high seriousness of, for example, Eisenhower or Carter. It is also a very emotional address—again, unlike the American fare.

However, the speech almost contradicts its tone by its heavy use of rhetorical schemes usually associated with formal epideictic oratory. And he uses those schemes to highlight what he feels are the many accomplishments of his government. The extent to which he personalizes his exposition, however, leaves the distinct impression that he sees these accomplishments as his, not Labor's. To the extent he implies as much, he is offering a very political farewell that refutes the basis for his removal from party leadership. He, of course, says nice things about Labor and about Gillard. However, he also seems to be raising the question as to why a prime minister with such accomplishments should be replaced. Some would even go farther and suggest that the emotionalism of the address was staged to evoke a positive public response toward his situation.

A review of the address will make these traits clear.

After offering general statements about his government, saying "I have given my absolute best . . . my absolute all," Rudd proceeds with statements beginning "I'm proud." There are twenty-four such statements, using the personal pronoun "I" forty-one times. These statements exhibit anaphora and, thus, call attention to themselves more. Rudd offers not an account of what his Labor government did; rather, he offers an account of what he did. Then, he offers his personal thank-yous, using "I" twenty-five more times before concluding. His language is not especially formal. Despite the anaphora, he maintains a casual style well-suited to the prevailing Australian culture.

His testament to his accomplishments is not random. He rises to a climax, evoking considerable *pathos* along the way. He begins with economic policy; then, he deals with infrastructure improvements, education, and health services. He dwells on the second, talking about technology, technical education, libraries, early education, a national curriculum, and university education (which he has expanded by fifty thousand seats). He then dwells in more detail on the third, discussing public hospitals, diagnostic services for cancer, and the National Organ Transplant Authority. On the last, he notes that he speaks as "somebody who borrowed someone else's aortic valve," sounding a note both personal and pathos-evoking. Then, he talks about housing, noting Labor's goal to half homelessness and how he made considerable progress on reaching this goal thanks to his wife, who had (as "first lady" of sorts) made this her special project.

After economic policy and social policy, Rudd moves to environmental issues, noting that his government ratified the Kyoto Protocol, which the Howard government had resisted. This discussion allows Rudd to transition to the international arena where Australia is now "on the global stage" "at the table of the G-20." Mixed metaphor aside, he casually notes that "having a place at the table when stuff goes wrong with the world is pretty useful."

Rudd concludes with the policy area he is the most proud of—Australia's treatment of its indigenous people. He notes the scholarships, job training programs, and actual jobs his government created for aboriginals. And he notes how he is especially proud to have seen through the parliament early in his government an apology to "the stolen generations." Their existence was something that had embarrassed the Howard government—to the point that it had tried to minimize the matter. Rudd, on the other hand, had wanted Australia to admit that, for decades in certain states, predominantly half-caste children were stolen from their aboriginal mothers and taken to special training centers where they were prepared for life (albeit a low-paid life) in white society. This policy was pursued because these half-caste children were felt to have enough white blood to be "redeemable." Also part of this embarrassing policy was the notion that, through further intermarriage, the aboriginal could be bred out of them.

As Rudd recalls the "big day" in Canberra that celebrated the apology, he begins to cry. He then, very personally, concludes his list of accomplishments he is proud of by saying "I'm less proud of . . . the fact that I have now blubbered."

The next part of the address contains more anaphora: this time, a succession of "thank-yous." These become increasingly personal. Rudd begins with the people of Australia, the Labor Party, those who made up his ministerial team, and the people of his district in Brisbane. Then, he thanks some members of his immediate staff. He comes near to concluding by thanking his family: "I thank my family, Therese, that's Jess, that's Nick, and the curly headed one with the good looks after his mother is Marcus. They are wonderful beings."

He then concludes his "thank-yous" by turning religious and thanking God:

> It is probably not the occasion for high statements of theology, but I'm sure you'd be disappointed if I didn't add something, given it's been the subject of comment over the years in which I've led this party. But to the great God and creator of us all, I thank him—or her—as well.

That comment, of course, implicitly offers Rudd's response to the criticism he had received for his introduction of religion into politics. The next part is ritual insofar as he pledges his loyalty to Labor and says his party deserves reelection because of all of the accomplishments he had claimed as his earlier in the speech. He notes that Labor is "led by a good Prime Minister." Then, he notes, "I mean Julia, not me, because I'm still the Prime Minister." He tensely jokes about how, for fifteen more minutes, he will be Prime Minister but not leader of the Labor Party. He says, "watch out because we can do things" during the quarter hour. "Anything could happen, folks," he adds.

He then talks about his future—not the retirement U.S. presidents usually talk about—but running for reelection for his seat in Brisbane. He, then, before he notes "we've got to zip," praises his wife again:

> She's always more succinct than me. And much better looking. The work Therese has done in the community is formidable. And whether it's disabilities, homelessness, UNICEF. This is a very good person. A very, very good person and one of life's eternal mysteries is why she ever married me in the first place. She is a very good person, as are these fantastic kids of mine.

The personal and the sentimental dominate the speech's end, but personal and sentimental notes are found throughout. As is the casual style, despite structuring devices more characteristic of formal rhetoric. The combination could be jarring, creating a tension; instead, I would suggest the combination is disarming, hiding—at least at first glance—how very political the speech is.

The speech, I would suggest, is designed to evoke sympathy for Rudd. The personal and pathetic touches in the address serve that end. The speech is also designed to make a strong case for Rudd's government. The long recitation of his government's accomplishments indeed makes one wonder, especially one not in Australia, why this man has been replaced as Labor's leader. And the only reason for his removal mentioned in the speech is his penchant for speaking about religion, and that certainly does not strike a listener as a proper basis for removal. In fact, the reason may strike a listener as patently unfair.

Commentators on American politics have argued over whether Hillary Clinton's tears during the 2008 New Hampshire presidential primary were genuine or staged. A similar debate rages over Kevin Rudd's "blubbering." If not dismissed as staged, then they represent a powerful indication of how strongly he felt about the cause of the nation's aboriginal people, especially about how "the stolen generations" had been treated by the Australian government. The tears, then, are a tribute to his sincerity as well as to his political morality. Rudd comes across as a sincere, moral man with a great many accomplishments in many policy areas. Why, I think Rudd wants his audience to ask, would one want to remove this man from his leadership position?

THE FAREWELL AS POLITICAL?

So, let us return to the genre of the farewell, voiced by a nation's political leader. In the United States, the genre seems to have been handled in a manner that avoids partisan politics. The Australian use of the genre, however, alerts us to the fact that there is nothing inherently nonpartisan about the genre. This realization does not simply point to the possibilities that the genre had different flavors in different nations and that the genre may have a different flavor in a parliamentary system than in the American system. This realization should cause scholars to reexamine the farewell genre even in this country to see if it may be a more politicized genre than usually thought.

Medhurst's work (1994) on the Eisenhower farewell should have already alerted us to the possibility. He refocuses attention away from Eisenhower's warnings and toward his repeated call for balance; and he contextualizes that call in Eisenhower's desire to counsel what he fears will be a brash Kennedy administration likely (in his view) to make mistakes in domestic and, especially, foreign policy.

This work and the general recognition, thanks to Rudd's example, that the genre can be quite political should suggest that other American farewells ought to be reexamined with the potential for stronger partisanship in mind. For example, was Carter's warning about special interest politics a statesman's warning or a swipe at how Reagan (and Republicans) was gaining funding and support through groups focused narrowly on particular issues or particular political philosophies? In addition, scholars might well want to embrace Nixon's two addresses on the occasion of his leaving office within the genre and mine those speeches for the way they are self-promoting, perhaps even taking somewhat restrained pot-shots at those who were, in his view, bringing down his presidency. There are, in fact, some striking similarities between Nixon's speeches and Rudd's. So, if Rudd's is a farewell—as it's labeled at least by the media—why aren't Nixon's?

CONCLUSION

Political communication scholars ought to look beyond the United States. If they do, they will find many fascinating "texts" to consider. There are speeches, advertisements, websites, and so on, well-worthy of serious scholarly consideration. There are, of course, many methodologies scholars might use. Using genre is but one. In the case of Rudd's farewell, using genre points to five interesting conclusions. First, the essence of the genre seems to be the ritualistic passing on of power and the positive review of the outgoing government's accomplishments. Second, the speech need not be as solemn or formal as the American examples suggest: in other political cultures, the speech can be "lighter" in style and tone. Third, the offering of warning—although *the* characteristic much American commentary has fixated on—may not be an essential characteristic. Fourth, the genre can do more overt political work than often thought. Fifth, the genre may not be limited to speeches delivered by sitting leaders as they ready themselves (and the nation) to yield to an elected successor. If Rudd's speech, delivered under other circumstances, is a farewell, then so is Nixon's as he left office and—perhaps—as he announces his pending resignation. This broadening of the genre further opens up the possibility of examples performing overt political work.

I earlier referred to a "back and forth" critical process. In one direction, the use of extant genre definitions based on U.S. discourse allows us to see dimensions of an international text that we might not note. In the other direction, what we see in examining an international text might result in a revising of the genre's definitions. In this case, both occur. We see both elements missing (warning) and elements, such as style, handled in a rhetorically different way that mixes formal structure with casual, personal language. We also see the genre being put to a political use more overt than what we *think* is the case in the United States. These differences should cause us to rethink whether a warning is an essential characteristic of the genre or just something Washington did and others in this country have imitated. Is there anything in the exigence of saying farewell that gives rise to a warning, or is it something Washington wanted to do that other American presidents have as well? These differences should also cause us to rethink how much beyond the ritualistic and the governmental the farewell speech can take a rhetor. Perhaps it is quite political, with the statesman-like pose but a veil. It would, of course, be more than just curious if there were political work being done by the speech. The political thrust could well be the point, something a political communication scholar most assuredly does not want to miss.

NOTE

1. Rudd's speech is quoted from *The Australian,* on line at www.theaustralian.com/au/full-transcript-of-kevin-rudds-farewell-speech/story-fn5vg.

TWELVE

Methodological Observations

One of the biggest barriers to studying political communication abroad is language. As I indicated in this book's preface, there is a reason for my focus on the Anglophone world beyond the fact that, as a scholar of discourse of various sorts, I study many of the countries in that world. That reason is language. As much as I might be interested in the politics in a place like—let's say—Russia, I could not undertake a study of the communication there because my Russian is not good enough to work intelligently with the texts. I could stumble through them, translating word-by-word, trying to arrive at a meaning that makes sense; however, such an approach would not alert me to the political nuances of the rhetors' word choices. And I think we would all admit that those nuances might be very important in any number of the messages.

So, if one were to study political communication in a foreign land, one methodological problem is that a researcher needs to have considerable facility in the language or languages of that land. However, there is another problem that many in the area believe to be relevant.

Our research does not occur in a vacuum. We build on both previous research and extant theory. That research is typically done in the United States: it looks at U.S. elections; it looks at the discourse of U.S. presidents; and so on. The question then is can this research base be used to frame questions about political communication elsewhere. Somewhat similarly, that theory is either rooted in U.S. discourse or in Western rhetorical theory. We have theorized about the farewell as a genre based on how American presidents have used the genre; we have theorized about matters such as intertextuality, polyphony, and the counterdiscursive—to name just three concepts—based on rhetorical theory originating in Czechoslovakia, the Soviet Union, and France. The question in this case is can this theory rooted in largely Western assumptions be used as a lens through which to consider political communication outside the West.

I want to answer these question by considering four cases: first, where the results of empirical studies or content analyses are used to frame research on international political communication; second, where the procedures used in these kinds of research are used to study international political communication; third, where the results of rhetorical studies focused on communication in this nation are used as a guide to analyses of foreign discourse; and fourth, where rhetorical (or critical) theory developed throughout the Western world (not just in the United States) is used as a lens through which to study international discourse. I choose these four cases because they strike me as the ones political communication research, should it be undertaken on acts and texts outside the United States, is most likely to find itself facing.

USING EMPIRICAL STUDIES

This first case is undoubtedly one of the most problematic. If, for example, one were to use the work by the late Linda Lee Kaid and her many former graduate students on videostyle in presidential campaigns to look at ads run in, let's say, Greece, one might conclude that ads there interestingly depart from the norm because they use more of a given technique than typical in such communication.[1] The assumption, of course, is that both the Greek political culture and media there match those in the United States. This assumption is likely not a safe one. It would probably be even less safe if the country under consideration were a third world one where democratic processes are relatively new, not ancient, and where media do not reach vast sections of the country.

A similar problem would arise if one were to take the results of a study of a political genre using Benoit's functional approach and use them in assessing how an example of the genre is used in Japan.[2] If the genre were an apology, for example, one would run smack into a culture in which matters such as giving offense, feeling shame, and apologizing play out very differently. Or if one were to extrapolate from the results of subjects turning dials during the 2012 Republican primary season debates to set up a study of responses to positive as opposed to negative or issue-related comments as opposed to image-related ones in debates in one of the former Soviet republics, one would be mixing a debate-savvy audience with one rather unfamiliar with open exchanges between candidates. The result of the mixing could well be conclusions about the latter that express surprise at very different data and look for an explanation in the candidates' discourse as opposed to in the very novelty of the political communication activity.

USING EMPIRICAL METHODS

The second case is somewhat less problematic, for here, it is the procedure, not the results, that are being used. Still, care is necessary, for the procedure might not fit the particular international situation. One can imagine a researcher needing to modify the lists of techniques used in defining videostyle. For one thing, the technology might be better in the United States than elsewhere (although the technology is surprisingly more up-to-date in places such as Jamaica than one might expect); for another, the level of government control may be higher or different—certain things permitted but not others. Benoit's three basic categories of acclaims, attacks, and defenses might translate more readily, as would the categories positive, negative, issue-focused, and image-focused. This is so because these categories are somewhat generic, not as culturally specific as the many videostyle characteristics. Still, care would be necessary in operationalizing terms. For example, what is not considered mildly negative in the United States might be considered very much so in a culture either more polite or a culture that, for example, finds violations of public trust far more objectionable than sexual transgressions.

USING RHETORICAL STUDIES

The third case moves us into rhetoric. The presumption among rhetoricians is that the art is universal. All rhetors strive for identification, as Burke tells us; many are in contexts featuring hegemony and necessitating the counterdiscursive, as Gramschi and Foucault tell us. Therefore, one ought to be able to use a rhetorical or critical analysis dealing with an American text as a springboard to studying an Italian one or a Thai one. I would suggest that this case is much like the second: care is necessary, not because the underlying theory is not generalizable but because the analyses have dealt with American texts that rise out of an American context and texts in a foreign land, although seemingly similar, are different in subtle ways. Does, for example, an inaugural function in Kenya is the same way rhetorically as in the United States? This is a question that I had to wrestle with in writing chapter 6. Does a farewell delivered by a prime minister or a party leader in a parliamentary system serve the same functions as a presidential farewell. This is a question that I had to wrestle with in writing chapter 11. The answer is almost always going to be "Yes and No," and it is crucial that the critic think about the reasons behind the "No" part and ascertain how these reasons might alter an analysis.

USING RHETORICAL THEORY

The fourth case involves rhetoric and criticism too, but it uses the theories as lenses, not the results of analyses as jumping-off points. Here, the critic is on relatively safe ground as long as he or she does not go too far beyond the Western world in which most of the theory we know and use has developed. Name the rhetorician: Aristotle, Cicero, Puttenham, Campbell, Burke, Perelman, Foucault, Bakhtin. In all cases, we are dealing with observations that are largely applicable to whatever discourse we are considering. Pathos is used throughout the discourse. Identification is a goal throughout. Power is relevant to varying degrees, but never irrelevant; the same is true for novelization, double-voicing, and the carnivalesque. I can safely ask about ethos in a text from Canada, just as I can inquire how novelized one from South Africa might be.

But what constitutes the Western world? One would not question the inclusion of Canada (chapters 1 and 2) or Australia (chapters 10 and 11), even though the native North American sections of Canada and the vast aboriginal stretches of Australia take us beyond the rhetorical "West." But what about the other nations considered in this study? Are they Western? Can Western rhetorical thought be applied to their discourse?

My answer is a cautious yes. All of them are multicultural, but the colonial period, even though it was relatively brief in Africa, affected education and government, both of which are strikingly British in both former African colonies and former Caribbean colonies. Even South Africa, which withdrew from the British orbit at the height of apartheid and, arguably, began to seem a tad German (reflecting the Afrikaners' German-Dutch-Huguenot origin), exhibits a politics that seems quite English. These Anglophone nations then are sufficiently Western to be studied using lenses derived from Western theorists, but a critic does need to be cautious. However, the caution needed in studying nations such as Jamaica or Kenya is not that much more than the caution that ought to be observed in studying Canada and Australia, which have definite non-Western elements. In fact, one might even say that some caution should be observed even here in the United States where the African American and Hispanic cultures demand slightly different rhetorical traditions as lenses than those that arise out of the mainstream "West" and where the Native American culture demands radically different ones. In other words, caution is generally necessary when using general theories.

Some have found the requisite methodological care to be a sufficient impediment to studying international political communication that they have turned to still more studies of our American campaigns or our American leaders. Although these additional studies are no doubt valuable, my suggestion to the political communication research community is to reach beyond the United States. Do so cautiously; do so exercising the requisite methodological care. But do so, for doing so expands the research community's significance. We will not be just illuminating what goes on in our nation but offering several audiences' insights into what goes on politically in the rest of the world. We would be doing so for the sake of knowledge, but also because we can then strike revealing comparisons between American praxis and that elsewhere and we might, in illuminating a foreign text, see a new way to illuminate a classic American one.

There are, after all, two rather different goals of political communication research, although one sometimes seems to get lost. The one all agree on is to build our understanding of political communication processes. A research project is good if it tells us more about, let's say, a political genre such as the apology or a political process such as communicating with voters between the end of the primary season and the late summer national conventions. Should this goal be the primary one in sight, then one can understand why research on political communication abroad might be pushed aside. What can political communication in Australia—let alone the Ukraine or Egypt—tell us about *our* processes? The answer is more than one might think if an adequate awareness of all of the relevant differences informs the research project. We can, for example, learn something about the farewell genre by examining its use elsewhere: we can see uses and characteristics abroad that may be obscured but nonetheless relevant here. The gut reaction, however, is that what's done abroad is so different that one should not bother if one's goal is to add to what we think we know about the political communication here.

Serving this first goal with international "texts" before one requires caution then, but caution does not mean that one should assume that conclusions drawn from practice abroad are useless in studying U.S. communication just as caution does not mean that one should assume conclusions, procedures, and theories derived from practice in the United States. are necessarily irrelevant abroad. Some in our research community evidently think so, but, with caution rooted in knowledge of political structures, practices, and cultures abroad, one can bridge the gap and learn a great deal about how political communication works—in general and in specific nations.

But there is the often ignored second goal, and that is to illuminate political "texts" because it is intrinsically valuable to know about the world's political actors and the communication they have engaged in. Using just a few examples drawn from this book, I would posit that it is valuable to know how Canadian Prime Minister Pierre Elliott Trudeau used the moments when he was in the limelight to advance his political goals. Not because he was a neighbor. Not because what he did might be what an American president did. But because Trudeau, as a national leader and as a player on the world stage, is worth studying. International players are worth studying for a variety of reasons—not just because they are "big" names. The same is true for events: the momentous are worth a look, but so are the curious. Bob Marley's political prominence is curious. That draws one's attention to how his message evolved. Gough Whitlam's response to his dismissal is curious: we, as rhetoricians, should want to know how he handled the exigencies of the situation, but we should, as scholars of public address, want to know why the speech is so very famous in Australia.

Our goal (second goal) as political communication scholars is, then, to illuminate the political communication that seems worth illuminating. Yes, if it is in the United States, it is easier to illumininate, but there is much that goes on elsewhere that is just as curious, just as interesting. We ought to grant that there are obstacles to studying these events, but we ought to push on because, as scholars, our goal should be to analyze what is important or interesting in the world, not just to increase our collective knowledge about some part of the American political process, but because there is intrinsic value to studying noteworthy political communication wherever it might occur.

The purpose of this modest book then has been to model what might be done. Different kinds of questions were raised. Different methods used. Some chapters have the feel of firm scholarship; others are more exploratory. The variety is deliberate because there are a variety of approaches one might take if one were to consider political communication in all of its international manifestations. There is also, of course, a wide variety of subjects to consider, in the Anglophone world and, if one has the language skills, beyond. My hope then is that these case studies, all of which look at an aspect of political communication that I would argue is both important and fascinating, inspire many, many more.

How many Canadian prime ministers are there? How many Caribbean and Africa nations? How many calypso artists in Trinidad? How much old media, not to mention new media? How many Australian parliamentary elections? There is much to be one—done with caution but nonetheless done by a political communication research community using its variety of theories and its variety of empirical and rhetorical tools.

NOTES

1. For example, Kaid and Johnston's *VideoStyle in Presidential Campaigns: Style and Context of Televised Political Advertising.*

2. For example, Benoit's *Accounts, Excuses, and Apologies: A Theory of Image Restoration Strategies* or Benoit, Blaney, and Pier's "Acclaiming, Attacking, and Defending: A Functional Analysis of U.S. Nominating Convention Keynote Speeches" in *Political Communication.*

Bibliography

Abrams. M. H. *The Mirror and the Lamp: Romantic Theory and the Critical Tradition.* New York: Oxford University Press, 1953.

Achebe, Chinua. *A Man of the People.* Oxford: Heinemann, 1966.

Armah, Ayi Kwei. *The Beautyful Ones Are Not Yet Born.* Oxford: Heinemann, 1979.

Attwood, W. *The Reds and the Blacks.* New York: Harper and Row, 1967.

Bakhtin, M. M. *Problems of Dostoevsky's Poetics.* Ed. and trans. by Caryl Emerson. Minneapolis: University of Minnesota Press, 1984.

Barnett, Ursula A. *A Vision of Order: A Study of Black South African Literature in English (1914–1980).* Amherst: University of Massachusetts Press, 1983.

Benoit, William L. *Accounts, Excuses, and Apologies: A Theory of Image Restoration Strategies.* Albany: State University of New York Press, 1994.

Benoit, William L., Joseph R. Blaney, and P. M. Pier. "Acclaiming, Attacking, and Defending: A Functional Analysis of U.S. Nominating Convention Keynote Speeches," *Political Communication* 17.1 (2000): 61–84.

Booth, Wayne C. *Critical Understanding: The Powers and Limits of Pluralism.* Chicago: University of Chicago Press, 1979.

Borstelmann, T. "'Hedging Our Bets and Buying Time': John Kennedy and Racial Revolutions in the American South and South Africa." *Diplomatic History* 24.3 (2000): 435–63.

Bothwell, Robert. *The Penguin History of Canada.* Toronto: Penguin, 2006.

Brink, Andre. *A Dry, White Season.* London: W. H. Allen, 1979.

Brystrom, Dianne G., Mary Christine Banwart, Lynda Lee Kaid, and Terry A. Robertson. *Gender and Candidate Communication: VideoStyle, WebStyle, NewsStyle.* New York: Routledge, 2004.

Burke, Kenneth. *Attitudes toward History.* Berkeley: University of California Press, 1984.

———. *Language as Symbolic Action: Essays on Life, Literature, and Method.* Berkeley: University of California Press, 1966.

———. *A Rhetoric of Motives.* Berkekey: University of California Press, 1950.

Campbell, Karlyn Kohrs, and Kathleen Hall Jamieson. *Deeds Done in Words: Presidential Rhetoric and the Genres of Governance.* Chicago: University of Chicago Press, 1990.

———. *Presidents Creating the Presidency: Deeds Done in Words.* Chicago: University of Chicago Press, 2008.

Campbell, Kim. *Time and Change: The Political Memoirs of Canada's First Woman Prime Minister.* Toronto: Doubleday, 1996.

Charland, Maurice. "Constitutive Rhetoric: The Case of the People Quebecois." *Quarterly Journal of Speech* 73 (1987): 133–51.

Coetzee, J. M. *Waiting for the Barbarians.*London: Secker and Warburg, 1980.

Davis, G. "No Ordinary Magic." *Electronic Mail and Guardian,* July 18, 1996. www.mg.co.za/mg/news/97jul2/18jul-mandela.html.

Dawes, Kwame. *Bob Marley: Lyrical Genius.* London: Sanctuary, 2002.

DiEugenio, J. "Dodd and Dulles vs. Kennedy in Africa." *Probe* 6.2 (1999). www.ctka.net/pr199-africa.html.

English, John. *Citizen of the World: The Life of Pierre Elliott Trudeau.* Vol. 1. Toronto: Knopf Canada, 2006.

———. *Just Watch Me: The Life of Pierre Elliott Trudeau.* Vol. 2. Toronto: Knopf Canada, 2009.

Fisher, Walter R. "Clarifying the Narrative Paradigm." *Communication Monographs* 5 (1989): 55–59.

———. *Human Communication as Narration: Toward a Philosophy of Reason, Value, and Action.* Columbia: University of South Carolina Press, 1987.

———. "Narration as a Human Communication Paradigm: The Case of Public Moral Argument," *Communication Monographs* 51 (1984): 1–23.

———. "The Narrative Paradigm: An Elaboration." *Communication Monographs* 32 (1985): 347–68.

Flesch, R. *The Art of Clear Thinking.* New York: Harper, 1951.

Franklyn, Delano, ed. *Michael Manley: The Politics of Equality.* Kingston, Jamaica: Delano Franklyn, 2012.

Frentz, Thomas S., and Janice Hocker Rushing. "Integrating Ideology and Archetype in Rhetorical Criticism, Part II: A Case Study of *Jaws.*" *Quarterly Journal of Speech* 79 (1993): 61–82.

Grattan, Michelle, ed. *Australian Prime Ministers.* 2nd ed. Sydney: New Holland, 2008.

Gutgold, Nichola D. *Almost Madam President: Why Hillary Clinton "Won" in 2008.* Lanham, MD: Lexington, 2009.

Hadland, A., and J. Rantao. *The Life and Times of Thabo Mbeki.* Rivonia: Zebra Press, 1990.

Hart, Roderick P. "Absolutism and Situation: Prolegomena to a Rhetorical Biography." *Communication Monographs* 43 (1976): 204–28.

———. *Campaign Talk.* Princeton, NJ: Princeton University Press, 2000.

———. "The Language of the Modern Presidency." *Presidential Studies Quarterly* 14 (1984): 249–64.

———. *Verbal Style and the Presidency.* Orlando, FL: Academic Press, 1984.

———. "Systematic Analysis of Political Discourse: The Development of DICTION." In K. Sanders, L. Kaid, and D. Nimmo, eds., *Political Communication Yearbook: 1984.* Carbondale: Southern Illinois University Press, 1985, 97–134.

———. "Of Genre, Computers, and the Reagan Inaugural." In H. Simons and A. Aghazarian, eds., *Form, Genre, and the Study of Political Discourse.* Columbia: University of South Carolina Press, 1986, 278–98.

———. *The Sound of Leadership: Presidential Communication in the Modern Age.* Chicago: University of Chicago Press, 1987.

———. *Diction 4.0: The Text-Analysis Program.* Thousand Oaks, CA: Scholari, 1997.

———. "Redeveloping DICTION: Theoretical Considerations." In M. West, ed., *New Directions in Computer Content Analysis.* New York: Ablex, 1998.

Jamieson, Kathleen Hall. *Beyond the Double Bind: Women and Leadership.* New York: Oxford University Press, 1995.

———. *Eloquence in an Electronic Age: The Transformation of Political Speechmaking.* New York: Oxford University Press, 1988.

Johnson, H. *People in Quandries: The Semantics of Personal Adjustment.* New York: Harper, 1946.

Kaid, Lynda Lee, and Anne Johnston. *VideoStyle in Presidential Campaigns: Style and Context of Televised Political Advertising.* Westport, CT: Greenwood, 2001.

Katriel, T., and A. Shenhar. "Tower and Stockage: Dialogic Narration in Israeli Settlement Ethos." *Quarterly Journal of Speech* 76 (1990): 359–81.

Lakoff, George. *Moral Politics: What Conservatives Know That Liberals Don't.* Chicago: University of Chicago Press, 1996.

———. *Women, Fire, and Dangerous Things: What Categories Reveal About the Mind.* Chicago: University of Chicago Press, 1987.

Lakoff, George, and Mark Johnson. *Metaphors We Live By.* Chicago: University of Chicago Press, 1980.

Laxer, James, and Robert Laxer. *The Liberal Idea of Canada: Pierre Trudeau and the Question of Canada's Survival.* Toronto: Lorimer, 1977.

Lodge, Thomas. *Politics in South Africa: From Mandela to Mbeki.* Bloomington: Indiana University Press, 2002.

Mabry, M. "Up from the Ashes." *Newsweek*, November 30, 1998, 36–38.

Macintyre, Stuart. *A Concise History of Australia*. Cambridge: Cambridge University Press, 1999.

Manuel, Peter. *Caribbean Currents: Caribbean Music from Rumba to Reggae*. Philadelphia: Temple University Press, 1995.

McDonald, Kenneth. *His Pride, Our Fall: Recovery from the Trudeau Revolution*. Toronto, Key Porter Books, 1995.

Medhurst, Martin J. "Reconceptualizing Rhetorical History: Eisenhower's Farewell Address." *Quarterly Journal of Speech* 80 (1994): 195–218.

Muehlenbeck, T. "John F. Kennedy's Courting of African Nationalism." web.jmu.edu/history/mhr/muehlenbeck/muehlenbeck-paper.doc. (An online summary of author's PhD dissertation.)

Naipaul, V. S. *A Bend in the River*. London: Knopf, 1979.

Nelson, A. K. "President Kennedy's National Security Policy: A Reconsideration." *Reviews in American History* 19.1 (1991): 1–14.

Noer, T. J. "The New Frontier and African Nationalism: Kennedy, Nkrumah, and the Volta River Project." *Diplomatic History* 8.1 (1984): 61–80.

Panton, David. *Jamaica's Michael Manley: The Great Transformation (1972–1992)*. Kingston, Jamaica: LMH Publishing, 1993.

"The Report Card." *Electronic Daily Mail and Guardian*, December 23, 1998. www.mg.co.za/mg/news/98dec2/23/23dec-reportcard.html.

"The Report Card for the Cabinet of '97." *Electronic Mail and Guardian*, December 24, 1997. www.mg.co.za/mg/news/97dec2/24dec-report.html.

"Report Card on the Cabinet." *Electronic Mail and Guardian*, December 31, 1996. www.mg.co.za/mg/news/96dec2/31-dec-remandela.html.

Rushing, Janice Hocker. "Evolution of 'The New Frontier' in *Alien* and *Aliens*: Patriarchal Co-optation of the Feminine Archetype." *Quarterly Journal of Speech* 75 (1989): 1–25.

———. "Mythic Evolution of 'The New Frontier' in Mass Mediated Rhetoric." *Critical Studies in Mass Communication* 3 (1986): 265–97.

———. "The Rhetoric of the American Western Myth." *Communication Monographs* 50 (1983): 14–34.

Rushing, Janice Hocker, and Thomas S. Frentz. "Singing Over the Bones: James Cameron's *Titanic*." *Critical Studies in Media Communication* 17 (2000): 1–28.

Sabato, Larry. *Feeding Frenzy: Attack Journalism and American Politics*. Baltimore: Lanahan, 2000.

Sampson, Anthony. *Mandela: The Authorized Biography*. New York: Knopf, 1999.

Schlesinger, Arthur M. *A Thousand Days: John F. Kennedy in the White House*. Boston: Houghton Mifflin, 1965.

Scult, A., M. C. McGee, and J. K. Kuntz. "Genesis and Power: An Analysis of the Biblical Story of Creation." *Quarterly Journal of Speech* 72 (1986): 113–33.

Shava, Piniel Viriri. *A People's Voice: Black South African Writing in the Twentieth Century*. Athens: Ohio University Press, 1989.

Sheckels, Theodore F. *The Lion on the Freeway: A Thematic Introduction to Contemporary South African Literature in English*. New York: Peter Lang, 1996.

———. "The Rhetoric of Thabo Mbeki on HIV/AIDS: Strategic Scapegoating." *Howard Journal of Communications* 15.2 (2004): 69–82.

Sheckels, Theodore F., ed. *Cracked But Not Shattered: Hillary Rodham Clinton's Unsuccessful Campaign for the Presidency*. Lanham, MD: Lexington, 2009.

Sheckels, Theodore F., Nichola D. Gutgold, and Diana B. Carlin. *Gender and the American Presidency: Nine Presidential Women and the Barriers They Faced*. Lanham, MD: Lexington, 2012.

Shriver, J. S. *Point of the Lance*. New York: Harper and Row, 1964.

Ward, Russell. *The Australian Legend*. 2nd ed. Melbourne: Oxford University Press, 1965.

White, Timothy. *Catch Fire: The Life of Bob Marley*. 2nd ed. New York: Holt, 2006.

"With Bobby in Darkest Africa." *Time*, June 17, 1966.

Wofford, Harris. *Of Kennedys and Kings: Making Sense of the Sixties*. Pittsburgh: University of Pittsburgh Press, 1992.

Woods, Donald. *Asking for Trouble: Autobiography of a Banned Journalist*. London: Peter Smith, 1981.

———. *Biko*. London: Paddington, 1978.

Wrong, Michela. *It's Our Turn to Eat: The Story of a Kenyan Whistle-Blower*. New York: Harper, 2009.

Index

About the Author

Theodore F. Sheckels is professor of English and communication studies at Randolph-Macon College in Ashland, Virginia. He has authored, coauthored, edited, or coedited both textbooks and scholarly studies in the political communication field including *When Congress Debates* (2000), *Maryland Politics and Political Communication, 1950–2005* (2006), *Cracked But Not Shattered: Hillary Rodham Clinton's Unsuccessful Campaign for the Presidency* (2009), and *Gender and the American Presidency: Nine Presidential Women and the Barriers They Faced* (2012). He has also published studies of Canadian, South African, and Australian literature and film including *The Lion on the Freeway: A Thematic Introduction to Contemporary South African Literature in English* (1996), *Celluloid Heroes Down Under: Australian Film, 1970–2000* (2002), *The Island Motif in the Fiction of L. M. Montgomery, Margaret Laurence, Margaret Atwood, and Other Canadian Women Writers* (2003), and *The Political in Margaret Atwood's Fiction: The Writing on the Wall of the Tent* (2012). He is the former president of the American Association of Australian Literary Studies and the current president of The Margaret Atwood Society.

Lightning Source UK Ltd.
Milton Keynes UK
UKOW042335131112

202147UK00007B/24/P